Praise for *The Empowerment Mindset* . . .

"Following Calvin Helin's very practical advice, we learn how to fill a half-full cup the rest of the way. He guides us in how to see that cup and overcome self-inflicted stuck points, whether from low self-esteem, peer pressure, or missing our inherent potentials. Aimed at everyman and everywoman, he helps us recognize that successful adapters, not the fittest, are the ones who succeed."

—Walter Beebe
President, New York Open Center

"*The Empowerment Mindset* not only is a pleasure to read but is written with a rare lyrical brilliance. I can say from personal experience that Calvin Helin 'walks the walk' of his empowerment philosophy."

—Kathleen Walker
Attorney, Vancouver Family Law

"Calvin Helin, in revealing the true path to prosperous living, has provided an opportunity for us to achieve our desires and dreams. *The Empowerment Mindset* is a tool for fixing the broken parts of our lives."

—Jimmy W. Arterberry, THPO
Comanche Nation

"A fundamental teaching of indigenous cultures urges individuals and communities to take responsibility to uphold healthy cosmic interrelations. In a world of dependency, imbalance, and cultural and political marginalization, Helin shows how the wisdom of the elders gives the gift of empowerment and future well-being."

—Duane Champagn, professor of sociology and American Indian studies, member of the Turtle Mountain Band of Chippewa, and author of *Notes From the Center of Turtle Island*

"Calvin Helin has provided a road map for those who have been challenged by misfortune to obtain happiness and success in their lives. He does so in a compassionate and nonjudgmental manner. This is not just another how-to guide but a gift from the heart."

—Kelly MacDonald
Attorney

"It is rare, indeed, for a voice of importance to arise and rarer still to have it penetrate and be heard above the ever undulating tide of cacophonous chatter. The voice of Calvin Helin is being heard and understood at large, so much so that he has established himself as one of the leading social commentators of our time."

—Michael Brotchie
Attorney

THE EMPOWERMENT MINDSET

LAWS OF EMPOWERMENT

1. To change our lives for the better, we must first accept responsibility for everything we think, say, and do, as well as cultivate attitudes and values that help us adapt to whatever situation arises.

2. We can choose to be victims of negative emotions, toxic thoughts, and self-defeating behaviors, or we can take responsibility for our lives and consciously counter the forces of mental and emotional sabotage.

3. We can improve our lives by recognizing the limitations imposed on us by our inflated egos and by practicing humility.

4. Nothing can be gained from dwelling on the uncertain nature of reality or focusing on things we cannot change. To shape the future we desire, it is best to accept life with an open mind, prepare to adapt to any change, and focus on factors that are under our control.

5. Our conscious minds can purposely program our subconscious minds to help us reach our goals through visualization, commitment and reinforcement, emotionalization, believing, and actualization.

6. To succeed, we need to draw on the resources of our hearts and spirits, so that we are always open to learning, are prepared to adapt to any new situation, and have the courage to take positive and decisive action.

7. Changing our lives means changing our thoughts. Our thoughts are the most critical link in the chain of factors that determine our destinies.

8. Empowering ourselves to achieve greater success means harnessing the power of values and attitudes that support our endeavors and help us achieve our goals.

9. Hard work and sustained efforts are necessary to achieve success. In everything we do, the rewards we receive are equal to the efforts we invest.

10. To control our destiny, we discover our life's purpose and develop a strategic plan for making our wishes a reality. In so doing we become the authors of our own success.

THE
EMPOWERMENT
MINDSET

SUCCESS THROUGH SELF-KNOWLEDGE

CALVIN HELIN

Published by:

Canadian editor: Peter C. Newman
US editor: Ellen Kleiner
Cover design: Hugh Syme
Book design and production: Angela Werneke
Illustrations: Bill Helin
Diagrams: Angela Werneke

Figure 2.1 photo © michelangelus / Fotolia.com
Figure 15.2 photo © PhotoStocker / Fotolia.com

Printed and bound in the United States of America

Publisher's Cataloging-in-Publication Data

1 3 5 7 9 10 8 6 4 2

To Cree elder Wopstegwan you Kiyew (Billy Jo Takaro),
for the wise counsel and excellent medicine
he has provided to me and so many others,
and to his wife Geraldene Takaro,
whose happy attitude, generosity, and warm heart embody
the empowerment mindset

ACKNOWLEDGMENTS

I would like to acknowledge the support of the following people: Kelly MacDonald, Elaine (Gosselin) Falstead, Dave Tuccaro Jr., and Kathleen Walker—whose collective encouragement and example, in the midst of their own very trying times, is living proof that the empowerment mindset exists in the hearts and souls of many. I am also grateful for the support of John and Inez Helin, Pat and Barb Helin, Greg and Fong Millbank, Te Taru White, Pamela J. Hoiles, Rob Hunt, Darrell Beaulieu, Dave Tuccaro, Simon Jackson, Italia Gandolfo, Spencer Proffer, and Tony Mayer. As well, I would like to thank internationally renowned artist Bill Helin for the beautiful artworks provided throughout the book, celebrated artist Hugh Syme for the fantastic cover, graphic designer Angela Werneke for her interior book work, and last but by no means least, editors Peter C. Newman and Ellen Kleiner for their collective expertise, suggestions, and consummate artistry.

CONTENTS

List of Illustrations 11

Preface 15

Introduction 17

PART I. FOUNDATIONS

CHAPTER 1. *Harnessing Our True Power* 27
CHAPTER 2. *Addressing Negative Emotions and Toxic Thoughts* 33
CHAPTER 3. *The Limitations of Ego* 45
CHAPTER 4. *Adapting to Change As the Law of Growth* 49
CHAPTER 5. *Developing and Maintaining a Mind of Reinvention* 57
CHAPTER 6. *The Open Heart Attitude* 63
CHAPTER 7. *Growing by Giving* 71
CHAPTER 8. *Understanding the Conscious and Subconscious Minds* 75
CHAPTER 9. *The Power of the Human Spirit* 91
CHAPTER 10. *Fear, Failure, and Risk* 97

PART II. TAKING ACTION

CHAPTER 11. *From Thoughts to Empowerment* 105
CHAPTER 12. *Empowerment Fundamentals* 121
CHAPTER 13. *Overcoming Psychological Barriers* 133

PART III. DEVELOPING A STRATEGIC PLAN

CHAPTER 14. *Understanding Strategic Planning* 141
CHAPTER 15. *Discovering Our Life's Purpose* 147
CHAPTER 16. *Developing a Strategic Vision* 153
CHAPTER 17. *Establishing Goals* 159
CHAPTER 18. *Making a Strategic Plan* 165

Conclusion: The Empowerment Mindset As a Way of Life 211

Notes 215

Bibliography 221

Index 225

ILLUSTRATIONS

Infinite Mystery 12

Catch a Star 22

Spirit Lifters at Work 69

Little Ol' Joe 92

Demons of Pain 94

Key to Empowerment 138

Learning with Grandpa 208

Infinite Mystery

A PRAYER

Infinite Mystery
Murky night
Great obscurity
Beyond sight

Falling leaf
Stormy sea
Mystical cosmos
I make my plea.

O Great Spirit
Hear me speak
In the darkness
The way I seek

Climb the mountain
Ford the stream
Rising higher
To reach my dream.

Mighty Power
I do confess
The plan eludes
For my success.

A breath of wind
The sun's embrace
Searching heaven
For rightful place.

Light of rapture
Need to find
With compassion
And lucid mind.

Sacred Being
At your feet
The war to win
No retreat.

PREFACE

I was raised in poverty on a remote Native American Tsimshian tribal reserve located on the northwest coast of Canada. As a young boy, it seemed that members of my tribe—and indigenous people in general—endured considerable hardship and lived with a great deal of dysfunction in their lives. As I traveled through life, however, it became clear to me that people from all cultures could become trapped by a pattern of habitual failure, not just those raised in indigenous communities. I witnessed people holding on to negative emotions and toxic thoughts, sabotaging themselves both mentally and emotionally. In this way, they became victims of emotions like worry, fear, jealousy, sadness, resentment, guilt, shame, and frustration, yet blamed others for the results of their own self-destructive behaviors. As I observed such self-sabotage, I became committed to creating solutions that would help others find more constructive and fulfilling ways to attain success and happiness in their lives.

From my research, writing, and life experiences, I have come to understand that it is not possible to simply give material assistance to people and expect them to do well in the long run. Instead, people need and, ultimately, desire the knowledge that will allow them to help themselves and feel empowered in their lives. People must comprehend how they got to where they are and learn to get to where they want to be. They must assume complete responsibility for their lives, face their fears, and adopt attitudes that will release their potential to create the lives they desire.

The purpose of this book is to show a way to greater success and happiness through the adoption of what I call the "empowerment mindset"—a way of living that empowers people to take charge of their lives. It guides readers through a series of processes, such as accepting and adapting to change, facing fear and failure, harnessing the power of values and attitudes, discovering a life's purpose, and developing a strategic vision and plan for the future. In addition, it addresses accessing the power of perhaps our greatest asset—the human spirit—and what it means to become a spiritual warrior. In short, this book seeks to empower people to alter their personal circumstances so they can achieve their goals and experience greater fulfillment. It is with both humility and gratitude that I offer *The Empowerment Mindset* to all those who wish to transform their lives now characterized by frustration, helplessness, and victimhood to lives that instead reflect happiness, success, and genuine empowerment.

INTRODUCTION

I shall be telling this with a sigh
Somewhere ages and ages hence:
Two roads diverged in a wood, and I—
I took the one less traveled by,
And that has made all the difference.

—Robert Frost

During their lives, people often regret not having pursued certain dreams or, having failed to achieve their ambitions, feel unfulfilled. Many aspire to be great artists, athletes, writers, actors, entrepreneurs, musicians, businesspeople, or scientists, while others simply want to be good parents or life partners, escape poverty, or help the less fortunate. However, frequently people find that their loftier goals remain unreachable—an outcome as true for those of privilege and wealth as for those mired in poverty.

Despite their circumstances, most people want essentially the same things out of life—health, success, happiness, relationships that help them feel loved and valued, work that allows them to focus on their passions, and sufficient resources to care for themselves and their families. But instead of persistently pursuing their goals they often settle for what life hands them, accepting mediocrity or failure rather than earning their rightful destinies. They develop a fatalistic view that their paths in life are predetermined and unalterable. They soldier on, continuing to do the same things and think the same thoughts, thus ensuring that they will never deviate from their frustrating course. While such determination may be generally admired, it is folly to maintain a fatalistic view in the face of habitual failure. Instead, people must understand that their character and circumstances are continuously evolving. Whenever they choose to, they can reinvent themselves through the thoughts they think, the emotions they feel, the images they visualize, and the actions they take.

Some common pitfalls on the road to success are negativity, self-doubt, fear, misinformation, laziness, and cowardice. Like Cowardly Lion in L. Frank Baum's *The Wonderful Wizard of Oz*, our lack of courage can make us afraid to follow a risky path or reluctant to embark on unfamiliar actions that may be needed to achieve success.

Instead of taking "the road less traveled," which could lead to realized ambition, we often take the easier, traveled road. For many people, this leads to negative emotions and toxic thoughts that make them dance their lives away in a fiery ring of hate, jealousy, blame, victimhood, learned helplessness, depression, and sometimes lateral violence. Negative emotions and toxic thoughts drain vitality and undermine self-confidence and self-worth, causing people to negate potentialities and say such things as "I can't" or "It won't make a difference anyway." Since it is often difficult to accept the shame to which such attitudes lead, the result is often further blaming, bitterness, and sense of being a victim—a self-destructive state of mind I call the "woulda, shoulda, coulda syndrome," or the WSC syndrome, which inevitably results in failure and despair. Individuals gripped by the WSC syndrome believe they are victims and deserve pity, which results in blaming others or outside conditions for their failures or unhappiness, leading them say such things as "I would have (should have, could have) done that if it had not been for my partner (parents, friends, the government, the president, the weather)."

WSC Syndrome

A self-destructive state of mind based on negative emotions and toxic thoughts that causes individuals to think they "woulda, shoulda, coulda" achieved a goal and blame themselves and others for their lack of success and unhappiness, inevitably leading to repeated failure, desperation, and victimization.

However, with knowledge about the human condition, those who are prepared to face their fears and are committed to the hard work required to transform their lives can transcend the WSC syndrome (or any other self-defeating behavior pattern) and attain greater fulfillment. This book outlines how to gain such knowledge through developing the "empowerment mind-set." The empowerment mindset is a state of mind in which individuals recognize the potential power they have over their lives; confront their fears; take ownership of their problems; accept responsibility for their actions; adopt positive thinking, attitudes, visualization, values, and actions; and implement a strategic plan to improve their lives. It offers tools to access the power we possess to help ourselves by accepting full responsibility for our lives, including everything we think, say, and do. To paraphrase the terminology of author Daniel Goleman, the empowerment mindset is about discovering our empowerment intelligence.[1]

Empowerment Mindset

A state of mind in which individuals recognize the potential power they have over their lives; confront their fears; take ownership of their problems; accept responsibility for their actions; adopt positive thinking, attitudes, visualization, values, and actions; and implement a strategic plan to improve their lives.

The ten laws of empowerment listed at the beginning of this book and placed individually at the end of strategic chapters serve as the foundation upon which the empowerment mindset is built. After years of observing what does and does not help individuals move out of the spiral of negative emotions and toxic thoughts that keep them from realizing their potential and reaching their goals, I developed these laws to assist them in creating the futures they desire.

Each chapter of this book explores a specific concept, attitude, outlook, practice, tool, or strategy that will further the reader's progress in developing an empowerment mindset. Chapters are followed by "Key

Points" that summarize—in question-and-answer format—the most essential ideas of the chapter. Figures are provided to assist in visualizing specific points or processes that will help in cultivating and maintaining an empowerment mindset. In addition, quotes, poems, and illustrations are included that will further inspire readers as they embark on their journey to reclaim and renew their lives. Unless otherwise stated, the poetry throughout this book is the author's and all artworks are by Bill Helin, the author's cousin.

People desiring to learn about and adopt the empowerment mindset must be willing to forge their characters in the furnace of life, resolving to withstand possible criticism, ridicule, adversity, and temporary failure. They must also be prepared to be open, generous, humble, hardworking, loving, and disciplined to gain the wisdom necessary to be successful. As Sufi mystic Rumi advised, change makes us better:

> You change one piece of ground to gold. Another you shape into Adam.
> Your work transforms essence and reveals soul.
> My work is forgetfulness and making mistakes.
> Change those to wisdom!
> I am all anger.
> Turn that to loving patience.
> You that lift the bitter earth into dough and baked bread to human energy,
> you that appoint a distracted man guide, a lost man prophet,
> you that arrange random patches in an elegant design,
> we've changed from our first condition a hundred thousand times,
> each unfolding better than the last,
> let our heart's eye see this: all changes coming from the changer.[2]

No matter where we are in our present lives or what we have done—good or bad—we possess the power to create the futures we desire as long as we persist in developing the tools and implement the steps along the way.

Taking this path requires a focused interest in the future and an understanding that we must take responsibility for creating our own successes.

In embarking on the journey to acquire knowledge for developing the empowerment mindset, we have nothing to lose and everything to gain. Whether we are trapped in economic dependency, caught in the WSC syndrome, or simply experiencing habitual failure and never reaching our envisioned goals, the empowerment mindset can provide the relief map to greater success, happiness, and more fulfilling lives. After acquiring the empowerment mindset, we will be able to teach our children that they have the same power to excel as everyone else—though it is only those with the courage to activate their innate ability who achieve and succeed.

Key Points

1. **What is the WSC syndrome and why is it harmful?**

   It is a self-destructive state of mind based on negative emotions and toxic thoughts that causes individuals to think that they "woulda, shoulda, coulda" achieved a goal and blame themselves and others for their lack of success and unhappiness, inevitably leading to repeated failure, desperation, and victimization.

2. **What is the empowerment mindset and how can it help people?**

   It is a state of mind in which individuals recognize the potential power they have over their own lives; confront their fears; take ownership of their problems; accept responsibility for their actions; adopt positive thinking, attitudes, visualization, values, and actions; and implement a strategic plan to improve their lives.

Catch a Star

I Can

Demons of doubt
Dogging the man
Lost to the might
The power of "I can."

Blinded by hate
Paralyzed by fear
Ever so timid
Chaos so near.

Always the victim
Who is to blame?
So much self-pity
Awash in self-shame.

Negative emotion
Too toxic a thought
Lost to the path
So eagerly sought.

Cleansing the mind
Opening the heart
Needed right now
A map to restart.

Mind of renewal
Adoption required
Time to transcend
Beyond the transpired.

Action essential
To follow this vision
Need to hit mark
With archer's precision.

Time to transform
Following this plan
Empowered with love
And knowing "I can."

PART I

Foundations

Chapter 1

HARNESSING OUR TRUE POWER

*Continuous effort—not strength or intelligence—
is the key to unlocking our potential.*

—WINSTON CHURCHILL

Overcoming adversity to achieve success requires adopting an empowerment mindset, which includes a willingness to change the habitual ways of thinking and acting that sabotage our success and the realization of our full potential. The empowerment mindset directs how to think and the attitudes to acquire, what to visualize, and what actions we can take to attain greater success and well-being.

American philosopher, psychologist, and educator John Dewey wisely observed, "The self is not something ready-made, but something in continuous formation through choice of action."[1] And poet Maya Angelou commented, "Living a life is like constructing a building; if you start wrong you'll end wrong."[2] We may have started "wrong" in life because we acquired destructive habits of thinking and behaving from our parents or everyday circumstances, and are blind to the harm they cause. But regardless of past or current life circumstances, there are three things people can control in forming the self—the thoughts they think, the images they visualize, and the actions they take. Thus, we have the freedom to change our lives if we cultivate the willingness and persistence to do so.

Author and speaker Dr. Wayne W. Dyer refers to our acquired, potentially destructive habits of thinking and behaving as "habitual mind" or "subconscious mind programming." Such programming consists of habitual thought patterns such as "I can't really help the way I am; after

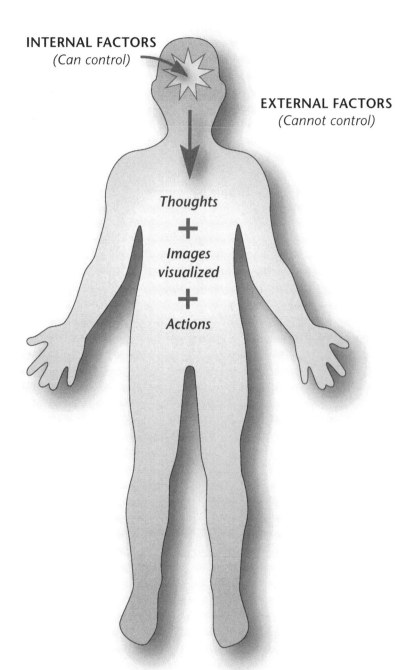

INTERNAL FACTORS
(Can control)

EXTERNAL FACTORS
(Cannot control)

Thoughts
+
*Images
visualized*
+
Actions

Figure 1.1 CONTROL FACTORS IN FORMING THE SELF

all, people can't change their DNA."[3] Not only do excuses like this sabotage our efforts to achieve success and happiness, but if we fail to overcome them we will likely pass them on to our children, ensnaring them in the same inescapable trap. However, we do not have to continue along a path of habitual failure. We have the power to make healthy choices for ourselves by changing our thoughts, visualized images, and actions so they will lead to success instead of failure.

The first step in making the switch from failure to success is to understand and accept that we are in charge—we are capable of utilizing our power to control our destiny. If we have experienced failures in the past, it is easy to believe that we are locked into a fate beyond our control and that there is no way to improve our circumstances regardless of how unsatisfying they may be. In fact, many people have become conditioned by overindulgent parents, well-meaning but poorly thought out government policies, or permissive modern attitudes to think that they are not responsible for themselves. However, this belief is a myth. If we buy into this myth, like the unwitting purchaser of a huckster's cure-all, our wallets and our well-being will take a hit. As stated in my book *The Economic Dependency Trap*, "only you can be responsible for the level of consciousness you bring to the party of life and how much you truly enjoy its festivities."[4]

Fundamentally, only from a position of personal accountability can we make the changes required to adopt and maintain the empowerment mindset. Life coach and author Brian Tracy observed that being responsible makes it impossible for us to remain angry or to blame other people for problems in our lives. The more we accept personal responsibility, the fewer negative emotions we will have to cloud our judgment and make us unhappy.[5]

The second step in making the switch from failure to success is turning on our internal "catalytic converter"—the part of us capable of reducing or eliminating toxic beliefs and self-defeating attitudes with which we have been operating—thereby activating our power. Brian Tracy suggested that one of the greatest revelations of his life was understanding that the primary reason some people were more successful than others was that they thought differently, made different decisions, and took different actions, so they got different results.[6]

Pioneer of personal-success literature Napoleon Hill called this the "success-conscious mind." He suggested that even those with a record of failure could attain a rapid-functioning mind, allowing them to achieve an impressive level of efficiency that did not depend on formal education.[7]

Alternatively, Dyer explains that to program ourselves for greater success we need to use the "creative conscious mind," the "close-to-the surface, non-habitual mind which makes endless decisions about what to wear, what to eat, what appointments you keep"[8] but has the power to do anything we instruct it to do and, through discipline, effort, and continual practice, can accomplish almost anything on which we focus.[9]

A major tenet of the empowerment mindset is that we can use our conscious minds to train, or "program," our powerful subconscious minds to help us achieve success and happiness. Unlike minerals, plants, and animals, humans have the ability to choose how to respond to stimuli, and in selecting our responses we alter our destiny. Austrian neurologist and Holocaust survivor Viktor E. Frankl, who recognized this innate capacity of humans, observed that the only freedom that cannot be taken from people is their right to choose their attitudes.[10] Each time we exercise this right we harness our inherent ability to modify our destiny and realize our highest potential.

One of the ways that the conscious mind can program the subconscious mind is through affirmations. Affirmations are positive statements describing a desired situation or result that, when repeated with attention and conviction, can influence the subconscious mind to alter our responses and help us achieve such outcomes.

Suggesting the results received in life are 10 percent what happens to us and 90 percent how we react to it,[11] author and educator Charles R. Swindoll proposes that the conscious mind can choose how to positively react to what happens so we can purposely achieve more successful results 90 percent of the time. Los Angeles psychotherapist Dr. Robert Redneck formulated a simple equation to succinctly illustrate this notion:

$$\text{Event} + \text{Response} = \text{Outcome}[12]$$

According to this equation, every outcome we experience is the result of an event plus a response to that event, implying that we have the power to affect outcomes by controlling our responses.

The empowerment mindset uses the knowledge that our responses depend on the thoughts we think, the images we visualize, and the actions we take to indicate that we are in charge of our destiny. And it allows us to cultivate attitudes and values that optimize our ability to respond to events in ways that help us succeed.

To alter our circumstances, we must be prepared to change ourselves. Adopting the empowerment mindset allows us to change ourselves to ensure that our attitudes permit us to adapt to circumstances to our greatest benefit. To adopt and maintain the empowerment mindset, we must accept full responsibility for everything we think, say, and do, and then activate our power by reducing or eliminating the toxic beliefs and self-defeating attitudes with which we have been operating, purposely cultivating attitudes and values that move us in a positive direction.

Key Points

1. How can the empowerment mindset help you harness your true power?

   It allows you to purposely cultivate attitudes, values, and a psychological disposition that optimize your ability to adapt to any situation. It can help you think the thoughts, visualize the images, and take the actions necessary to achieve more beneficial outcomes in your life.

2. What is "subconscious programming?"

   Programming made up of habitual thought patterns that people use to excuse or explain behavior that leads to repeated failure.

3. What is the "success-conscious mind?"

The conscious mind that has the power to do anything you instruct it to do.

4. What are affirmations and how can they help?

Affirmations are positive statements that describe a desired situation or result that, when repeated with attention and conviction, can influence the subconscious mind to alter your responses and help you achieve the desired outcome.

5. Why is self-responsibility an important aspect of the empowerment mindset?

Taking responsibility for yourself diminishes the possibility that you will blame others for your life circumstances and experience negative emotions likely to sabotage your ability to change yourself in beneficial ways.

Law of Empowerment 1

To change our lives for the better, we must first accept responsibility for everything we think, say, and do, as well as cultivate attitudes and values that help us adapt to whatever situation arises.

Chapter 2

ADDRESSING NEGATIVE EMOTIONS AND TOXIC THOUGHTS

Sooner or later, all of us must see that negative feelings
toward another person are like tossing dust at him
while the wind blows it against us.
It all comes back.

—VERNON HOWARD

The first step to adopt and maintain an empowerment mindset is to recognize the forces of personal sabotage and learn how to counter them. Without being recognized and countered, these negative forces can bring on a victim mentality and self-defeating behaviors that lead to learned helplessness; self-pity, blame, and envy; lateral violence; and depression. They can also lead to community- and group-conditioned negativity. In place of these nonproductive strategies, we must embrace self-responsibility and positive motivation to achieve success and happiness.

IMPACTS ON THE INDIVIDUAL

The mind is its own place, and in itself
Can make a Heaven of Hell, a Hell of Heaven.

—JOHN MILTON

Negative emotions and toxic thoughts—those that keep us from taking responsibility for our lives—are two of the greatest barriers to success and happiness. As author and philosopher James Allen once observed,

"Each of us is literally *what we think*…we are what we think. . . . If our mind has evil thoughts, we will suffer pain; if our thoughts are pure, joy will follow."[1]

Recent findings in the new area of embitterment research confirm that negative emotions can lead directly to physical illness since they "have the power to influence our biology [by releasing] more cortisol [which, like adrenaline, is a stress hormone] into circulation, which, in turn, can communicate with other body systems—the immune system, for example."[4] In other words, having a bitter attitude invites greater difficulties rather than improving our circumstances. No amount of negative emotions will correct unfavorable situations as they result only in additional emotional sabotage.

In this same vein, Brian Tracy pointed out that people become what they think about most of the time, so if their attitudes are largely critical and negative it should not be surprising to learn that they have many problems in their lives.[2] Author Joseph Murphy, PhD, DD, warned that millions of people are so psychologically and spiritually blind they are unable to recognize that by being hateful, resentful, or envious of others they secrete mental poisons which work to destroy them.[3]

Further emphasizing how our emotions and thoughts determine the qualities we experience, in his beautiful essay "Compensation" Ralph Waldo Emerson observed how we reap what we sow: "You cannot do wrong without suffering wrong. . . . Treat men as pawns and ninepins, and you shall suffer as well as they."[5]

However, despite the great power our thoughts and emotions have in determining outcomes in our lives many people fail to understand their force and thus continually sabotage themselves mentally and emotionally, unable to take charge of their circumstances. Mental sabotage occurs when people who wish to become successful and happy have self-perpetuating toxic thoughts that lead them on an emotional and psychological course capable of seriously impairing their well-being. For those who habitually experience failure and are trapped in the WSC syndrome, toxic thoughts

Figure 2.1 FORCES OF PERSONAL SABOTAGE

can take the forms of emotional insecurity about potential achievement or feeling undervalued in families or communities, resulting in a victim mentality. When interpreted against a backdrop of perceived victimization, neutral comments from any source can fuel even more toxic thoughts, leading to more feelings of anger, hurt, and powerlessness. This dynamic, in turn, reinforces lack of self-worth and fosters a perception of being seen negatively by society. In contrast, people who have substituted toxic thoughts with a positive view of themselves and their circumstances are less likely to adopt a victim mentality and more likely to experience success and well-being.

Emotional sabotage, on the other hand, occurs when the consequences of negative emotions, such as learned helplessness, self-pity, blame, jealousy, lateral violence, or depression manifest in self-defeating behavior. Learned helplessness surfaces in people who have learned to act helpless in unpleasant or harmful situations, after which not trying to improve their circumstances becomes habitual. Those who fall prey to learned helplessness often become inactive, hostile, and self-pitying, resulting in diminished self-esteem.[6] Unfortunately, this path to failure becomes justified by a self-looping story in which a past failure was the inevitable result of doing nothing. People preoccupied with dynamics of learned helplessness have difficulty moving forward in life. Blaming external causes for their unhappiness, they relinquish both their personal power and their access to internal resources that could help them change their circumstances.

Self-pity is said to be the most destructive of the nonpharmaceutical narcotics since it is addictive, gives momentary pleasure, and separates the victim from reality.[7] Self-pity also fosters a victim mentality since it can cause individuals to abdicate personal responsibility for their lives. Self-pity is intimately connected with the tendency to blame others or external forces for personal circumstances. Often people wrongly focus on their life partner, a parent, their friends, the government, or their employer as the source of their problems. Blaming then becomes a self-defeating thought pattern that inhibits progress toward goals. Likewise, self-pity also can trigger self-doubt and jealousy—additional negative forces that prevent people from adopting the empowerment mindset.

Lateral violence, another consequence of negative emotions, occurs when dominated people internalize feelings such as anger and turn on each other rather than confronting the system that oppresses them. Since they cannot strike out at their oppressors above them, their violence is directed laterally at their own family or group. Lateral violence is characteristic of individuals who live in slums and other impoverished environments that ensnare people in patterns of habitual failure. It is both a consequence of habitual failure and a cause of the downward spiral in social relations observed when larger, more powerful groups in control treat members of a minority group as inferior.

Depression, a common but often misunderstood mental disorder, is yet another way negative emotions and toxic thoughts can manifest. Although people of all ages and backgrounds can suffer from depression, it often occurs among those who experience habitual failure and the WSC syndrome because they have been unable to validate their self-worth by achieving success. Depression has been called the "spiritual territory of despair."[8] Andrew Solomon, author of *The Noonday Demon: An Atlas of Depression*, described depression as "An experience, overall, of finding the most ordinary parts of life incredibly difficult; finding it difficult to eat, finding it difficult to get out of bed, finding it difficult and painful to go outside, being afraid all of the time of being overwhelmed all the time. It's primarily an experience of sadness."[9] He further suggested that depression gives us a sharpened sense of how our negative internal self-talk really determines everything.[10]

While depression is serious, it can be reliably diagnosed and successfully treated. Interestingly, an emerging form of treatment for depression, called cognitive-behavioral therapy (CBT), emphasizes the impact of thoughts and attitudes on how people feel and what they do.[11] Recognizing that defining and achieving goals can positively affect a person's state of mind, cognitive-behavioral therapists "seek to learn what their clients want out of life (their goals) and then help their clients achieve those goals."[12] In some ways, this form of therapy parallels the empowerment mindset focus on achieving success through altering thought and behavior patterns.

COMMUNITY- AND
GROUP-CONDITIONED NEGATIVITY

People seem not to see that their opinion of the world
is also a confession of character.

—RALPH WALDO EMERSON

Some community and group dynamics can also condition members to respond to life challenges with negative emotions and toxic thoughts that lead to their inability to achieve success and happiness. For example, I was raised on a Native American reservation where, over generations, economic dependency had been enforced by government policy. All wealth came solely from the federal government and was controlled by an elite group consisting of an elected chief and council, effectively limiting individual members' power and potential for successful enterprise. While the situation is now changing, and more well-run communities with enlightened moral leaders are emerging, communities continue to exist in which members live in constant fear of retribution from those who control the wealth and every aspect of reservation life, limiting possibilities for personal development. In such situations, people feel they have no control over their lives, and feelings of powerlessness and frustration often manifest in alarming social pathologies. In milieus where group members who have similar views continually reinforce negativity, this collective negative outlook becomes accepted as normal, and people who grow up in such environments come to see life through a lens of negative emotions and toxic thoughts—a phenomenon I call community- and group-conditioned negativity.

The harmful dynamics of community- and group-conditioned negativity affect any group struggling to move constructively forward, such as those living in a ghetto, government agency workers, members of a social club, or a group of employees in a workplace. Community or group members can become like trees in a forest of negativity, unable to see the tremendous harm caused by living in such an unhealthy environment. Often the only alternative for those who wish to escape to a more positive environment and adopt an empowerment mindset is to leave. This is perhaps a major reason why in Canada over 70 percent of Native Americans wishing to improve their lives first leave their communities.

The individual members of groups caught in such destructive patterns often continually defeat the achievement of collective goals because the more positive individuals in the group are too timid to impose their opinions on more aggressive members who have more toxic thought patterns. The group members' attitude is the opposite of that of leader and winning football coach Vince Lombardi, who suggests that individual commitment to a group effort is what makes a team work, a company work, a society work, and a civilization work.[13]

It is easy to distinguish between the factions within such a group or community. The more progressive individuals are positive, cooperative, generally reasonable, and wish to create constructive change, while the others acknowledge the desirability of achieving goals but continually divert attention from them by coming up with excuses why the goals cannot be achieved. Frequently they employ forms of intimidation or suggest things that may sound reasonable but, on deeper examination, are designed to reinforce their own sense of importance, preserve privileges that such chaos allows them to enjoy, or demonstrate that they have power by preventing constructive action.

If we were to analyze the thought patterns of such individuals, we might find an underlying insecurity or an overdeveloped sense of entitlement. Their thought process might be: "These progressive people think they know every-

---

Community- and Group-Conditioned Negativity

A collective state of mind dominated by negative emotions and toxic thoughts that takes hold in a community or group that has been oppressed for so long that it oppresses its own members, undermining the ability of individuals or the collective to progress.

---

thing—certainly more than me—but I am not stupid. In fact, I know more than they do. I will show them what power I have by not supporting their goal." We might also uncover a self-defeating habit of thought that maintains: "I don't like that person. Whatever they are talking about can't, therefore, be good. I will not support it." Thus, rather than pursue collective goals these individuals undermine their own—and their group's—interests.

Many such individuals may not realize they have a habit of thought that is obstructing their interests. Instead, they may conclude that whatever they aspire to accomplish simply never works out. To free themselves from the grip of such negative thinking, they need to realize that their destiny begins with their thought patterns and that toxic thoughts can only lead to negative results.

Regrettably, there is a high likelihood that if such people don't realize the harm they are causing to themselves and others they will pass this enormous disadvantage on to their children and families. By harboring so much negativity, they essentially reinforce their track in a continuous loop of belligerence, unhappiness, and failure.

To demonstrate how damaging and infectious negative thought patterns can be, let me give you an example from my own personal experience. At one point in my life, I worked as a crew member on a large fishing boat. New to the ship, I was shocked by the behavior of the captain, who verbally abused the crew throughout the entire workday. This disrespect and mistreatment of the crew upset me. One day, however, one of the very old crew members said to me, "Don't worry about him. He behaves that way because that is the way his father treated him." This crew member's insight helped me understand why the captain behaved in such an obnoxious manner—his father's negative thoughts and self-defeating behaviors had been passed on to him, trapping him in a loop of abusiveness and unhappiness. It also allowed me to see that the negative baggage the captain carried was his problem, not mine—although one that unfortunately affected the morale of the crew.

While it is within our power to escape such a circular path of failure, we must make a conscious effort to do so. This involves assuming full responsibility for our lives, recognizing tendencies and limitations that may have been passed down to us by our ancestors, and taking the steps necessary to free ourselves from the dynamic of community- or group-conditioned negativity.

COUNTERING MENTAL AND EMOTIONAL SABOTAGE

*All that we achieve and all that we fail to achieve
is the direct result of our own thoughts. . . .
As we think, so we are: as we continue to think, so we remain . . .
the higher we lift our thoughts, the more upright and righteous we become,
the greater will be our success, the more blessed and enduring
will be our achievement.*

—JAMES ALLEN

Countering mental and emotional sabotage begins with accepting personal responsibility for all behaviors and outcomes in life. To succeed, we must purposely replace such negative emotions, toxic thoughts, and self-defeating actions with healthier emotions, thoughts, and actions. For example, if we constantly think about hating, then we should purposely think about loving. Author Napoleon Hill noted that eminently successful men such as Andrew Carnegie, Henry Ford, and Thomas Edison were not more intelligent than other men. Instead, their genius lay in their positive mental attitude, which made "their brain-power, not greater, but more efficient and more available than most others'."[14] Hill further contended: "A positive mind tunes in other positive minds [so that]… once I had accepted that great task and set my mind confidently toward it, I found my imagined obstacles simply melted away."[15]

The following is a list of five commonly used excuses, along with affirmations that counter them, to assist in eliminating negative emotions and toxic thoughts that might arise when we are seeking to escape the WSC syndrome and adopt an empowerment mindset.

1. I can't do it: *I can accomplish any task I set my mind to because I have a huge reserve of untapped potential, and I have not yet explored my vast abilities.*

2. People will make fun of me: *I am the only one who can change my future so the opinions of others are not important.*

3. I will fail: *I will seize this opportunity and pursue it to a successful end, but even if I should fail, the knowledge I will gain along the way will constitute a success.*

4. Everyone will be against me: *I am a good and decent person, and if the Creator is with me those who count will support me and those who do not don't matter.*

5. I am afraid to try: *It is natural to be afraid of failure, and although I am confident, I understand how failure can also be a great teacher.*

As we have seen, negative emotions and toxic thoughts lead to emotional and mental sabotage and prevent us from attaining happiness and success in our lives. They can rob us of our self-confidence, strip us of motivation, or, if left unchecked, lead to emotional and even physical illness. It is up to us, therefore, to recognize and address negative emotions and toxic thoughts in whatever form they take. No matter what we may have "inherited" from our families or communities in the way of habitual thinking or acting, we can learn to identify the forces of personal sabotage and learn how to counter them. (See my book *The Economic Dependency Trap* for further discussion on how to overcome personal sabotage.)

By adopting an empowerment mindset, we can consciously address our negative emotions and toxic thoughts and eliminate mental and emotional sabotage from our lives.

Key Points

1. **Name ways in which negative emotions and toxic thoughts can impact emotional and psychological health.**

   They can lead to learned helplessness; self-pity, blame, and jealousy; lateral violence; depression; and community- and group-conditioned negativity.

2. **How do negative emotions and toxic thoughts harm your ability to succeed and be happy?**

   Continually experiencing negative emotions and toxic thoughts can drain the energy and undermine the self-motivation you need to perform at a high level, resulting in negative outcomes.

3. **How is it possible to avoid or counter some of these problems?**

   By choosing to be more responsible, understanding how negative emotions and toxic thoughts can be damaging, and focusing on positive emotions and empowering thoughts.

4. **How do negative emotions and toxic thoughts impact communities or groups?**

   When negative emotions and toxic thoughts have existed a long time in a community or group, the resulting negative thinking of one or more individuals within that community or group can interfere with the fulfillment of goals based on collective interests. Also, the more aggressive members may dominate the group through intimidation or treat others roughly as a show of power.

Law of Empowerment 2

We can choose to be victims of negative emotions, toxic thoughts, and self-defeating behaviors, or we can take responsibility for our lives and consciously counter the forces of mental and emotional sabotage.

Chapter 3

THE LIMITATIONS OF EGO

*When a man is wrapped up in himself,
he makes a pretty small package.*

—JOHN RUSKIN

The ego can be one of the biggest obstacles people face in seeking to improve their lives by adopting the empowerment mindset. Perhaps the greatest fallout in this age of narcissism and self-indulgence is widespread self-absorption. Many people are so consumed by their own image of themselves that they cannot see, let alone understand, anything else or discern the danger of self-importance to their own well-being. The attitude of expectancy and sense of entitlement felt by such people would astound our grandparents, who were raised in a time when modesty was considered a virtue.

If we want to realize our greatest potential, we must first comprehend how the ego impacts our thinking, makes us behave, and keeps us from taking the steps necessary to improve our lives, and then learn how to break free from the prison of our inflated egos. One major problem individuals with inflated egos have is not comprehending that the ego, *a lens* through which we view reality, makes us think it is reality. This lack of discernment can distort reality and result in an exaggerated sense of self-importance and inability to empathize with others. Swiss psychiatrist Carl Jung was referring to this quality of the ego when he said that the ego *"is conscious of nothing but its own existence . . . is incapable of learning from the past, incapable of understanding the contemporary events, and incapable of drawing the right conclusions about the future . . .* eventually doom[ing] itself to calamities that must strike it dead."[1] [emphasis added]

Another challenge people with inflated egos face is difficulty in acknowledging their shortcomings. Lord Chesterfield once said, "Our own self-love draws a thick veil between us and our faults."[2] But we cannot fix problems unless we admit we have them. By contrast, the advantage people with humility have is that they are able to readily admit their faults and deal with them. Once we realize how our egos are preventing us from moving forward, we can make corrective changes and practice greater humility.

Additionally, people with inflated egos become averse to risk and therefore unable, because of fear of failure, to take actions required to invest in their true self-interest. Instead, they avoid anything that involves a potential for failure or that could make them look bad, and are reluctant to experience the unknown, as Deepak Chopra has observed.[3] However, if we want to escape the WSC syndrome and improve our lives we must be prepared to take some risks, which involves breaking out of the prison of the ego.

A further problem for people with inflated egos is that they often do not understand that their conceit is a turnoff for everyone around them. It's difficult, if not impossible, to remain engaged in a conversation with people who focus only on themselves. We like to deal with individuals who are genuinely interested in others. If we want others to support and assist us with our goals, we must be willing to support and assist others with theirs. This is exemplified by a story about an individual who sought counseling concerning a troubled marriage. After evaluating this person's circumstances, the counselor said, "Your marital problems will disappear when you love your partner more than you love yourself." If love for oneself is greater than the love for the other person, it blocks communication and the pathway to empathy.

Thus having an inflated ego can be an obstacle to communicating and empathizing with others. The drawback of having such an obstacle in our lives is particularly evident when we recognize that one of the greatest pleasures we derive as social beings is not from dreaming in isolation of a self-aggrandized image of ourselves but from sharing our humanity with others. Life is like a two-way radio—we have to be on the same frequency with others for our messages to be received and to receive their messages. People with big egos are one-way broadcasters who lack the capacity to receive anyone else's messages. Without the ability to communicate and empathize with others, life becomes a lonely, shallow, unhappy experience. We become like

Figure 3.1 IMPACT OF EGO

the castaway Robinson Crusoe, except that we have marooned ourselves on our island.

In our quest to adopt an empowerment mindset, escape the WSC syndrome, and achieve success and happiness in our lives, we must guard against an inflated ego that prevents us from obtaining an accurate view of reality, admitting our shortcomings so we can improve ourselves, taking necessary risks that could help us succeed, or communicating and empathizing with others. Because these tendencies may alienate us from people who could support and assist us in reaching our goals, to succeed we need to replace any exaggerated self-importance with a more realistic sense of ourselves and a more humane perception of others.

Key Points

1. **Name ways in which an inflated ego can undermine your ability to succeed.**

   It distorts reality, giving you an exaggerated sense of self-importance; it keeps you from acknowledging your shortcomings so you can improve your character; it makes you risk averse when you need to be taking chances to improve your life; it is an obstacle to communicating and empathizing with others.

2. **How can you diminish the impact of ego?**

   By practicing humility and having abundant love for those around you.

Law of Empowerment 3

We can improve our lives by recognizing the limitations imposed on us by our inflated egos and by practicing humility.

Chapter 4

ADAPTING TO CHANGE AS THE LAW OF GROWTH

Nothing that is can pause or stay;
The moon will wax, the moon will wane,
The mist and cloud will turn to rain,
The rain to mist and cloud again,
Tomorrow be today.

—HENRY WADSWORTH LONGFELLOW

In modern life, there is an increasing need to adapt to change if we are to grow and succeed. The idea of adapting to change as the law of growth is fundamental to the empowerment mindset. In Charles Darwin's time, the social structure, like the condition of every plant and animal, was thought to be divinely ordained—static and eternal. It is now popular for people to say that Darwin's contribution to knowledge is the idea that it is the fittest (the strongest and the smartest) who survive. However, what Darwin really emphasized was that *those most capable of adapting to change, whatever form it takes, have the best chance of surviving, not the fittest.* It is critical to understand the distinction between these ideas.

While our knowledge about reality has evolved exponentially since Darwin's time, most people still live their lives as if they were locked into an unchanging environment. In *Seven Life Lessons of Chaos,* authors John Briggs and F. David Peat suggest that the reason for this reluctance is the misconception taught from birth that reality is static.[1] They contend that our habits of mind and the supposed "facts" about the world learned from infancy distort our perception of reality.[2] Actually, in contrast to this perception of existence as fixed, reality is constantly in flux.

It is *not* the strongest of the species that survives, nor the most intelligent. It is the one that is most adaptable to change.

Figure 4.1 WHAT DARWIN ACTUALLY SAID

The dramatic rate of change in modern life is emphasized by the following facts:

◆ China will soon become the country with the most English speakers in the world.[3]

◆ The 25 percent of India's population with the highest IQs amounts to more people than the total population of the United States. In addition, India has more children who achieve scholastic honors than the United States has children.

◆ In 2010, the top ten jobs most in demand did not exist in 2004. We are currently preparing today's students for jobs that do not yet exist, using technologies that still have to be invented to solve problems currently unknown to us.

◆ The US Department of Labor estimates that today's learners will have had ten to fourteen jobs by age thirty-eight.[4]

The dramatic rate of technological change and its impact is underscored by the following facts:

◆ While it took radio thirty-eight years to reach an audience of 50 million, it took television thirteen years, the Internet four years, the iPod three years, and Facebook two years.

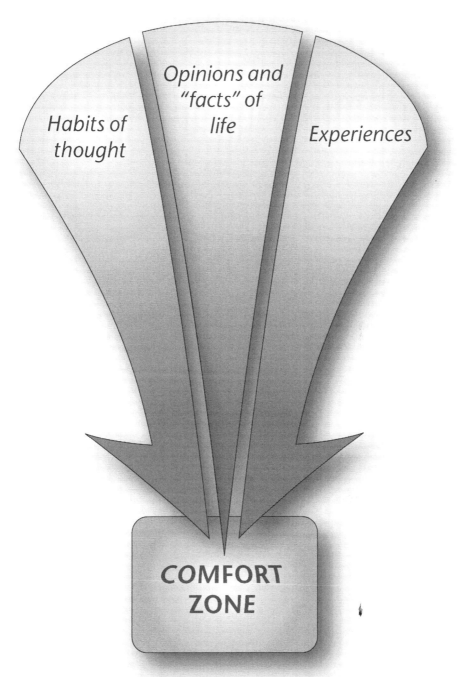

Figure 4.2 FACTORS CREATING A STATIC VIEW OF REALITY

- While the number of Internet devices in 1984 was one thousand, in 1992 it was one million, and by 2008 it had reached over one billion.

- It is estimated that one week's issues of the *New York Times* contain more information than someone living in the eighteenth century was likely to encounter in their entire lifetime.

- It is estimated that four exabytes (4.0×10^{19}) of unique information was generated in 2010, a figure that exceeds the entire body of information generated in the preceding five thousand years.

- The amount of technical information is doubling every two years. This means that half of what students embarking on a four-year technical degree learn in their first year of study will be outdated by their third year of study.

- It is predicted that by 2013 a supercomputer will be built that exceeds the computational capabilities of the human brain, and that by the year 2049 a computer costing $1,000 will have the capacity to exceed the computational capabilities of the entire human species.[5]

As these examples clearly demonstrate, the rate of change on the planet is increasing exponentially. To resist such change is to swim against the tide of reality. In *Managing Your Mind: The Mental Fitness Guide*, psychologists Gillian Butler and Tony Hope point out that even though the external world is constantly changing with many influences beyond our control we should understand that we are not powerless—we can alter our experiences by changing our reactions to external events.[6] Resisting change limits our responses to circumstances and opportunities (ensuring we remain stuck in a rut that often results in failure) when to succeed we need to accept that change is unavoidable and summon the courage necessary to adapt.

The problems many people face in adapting to change are fear of the unknown and overcoming the desire for comfort and complacency. Change entails uncertainty, and uncertainty can introduce fear and insecurity regarding perceived threats to safety and peace of mind. On the other hand, despite people's reasoning that if they just keep doing what they have always done they will be safe and life will be predictable, author Helen Keller noted, "Security is mostly superstition…[which] does not exist in nature. Avoiding danger is no safer in the long run than outright exposure. The fearful are caught as often as the bold."[7]

Life coach Brian Tracy underscores the idea that adaptation to change is the law of growth, suggesting that we must resist the natural tendency to become comfortable and complacent in work and lifestyles, and that we can escape our comfort zone and overcome our fears of helplessness and failure by setting big goals and then putting our whole heart into their accomplishment.[8]

Seeing adaptation to change as the law of growth helps us understand its importance for our success. No matter how difficult or challenging our lives may be, our success depends on accepting the need for change and believing that we have the power to adapt to change in our lives.

To transform our lives in a manner that furthers our aspirations, we must recognize and accept the changing nature of modern life; take the practical, necessary steps to be ready for change, such as saving money for a "rainy day"; approach change with a view toward managing it rather than fearing and avoiding it; and embrace the positive aspects of change, such as learning and growth. While uncertainty caused by change can result in uneasiness, it can also give birth to creativity, possibility, and hope. As author and poet Myrtle Reed noted, "Impermanence is the very essence of joy— the drop of bitterness that enables one to perceive the sweet."[9] The empowerment mindset requires a mind attuned to reinvention, which we can only attain by embracing the potential of change to benefit our lives.

Key Points

1. **Why is it harmful to see reality as static if you are trying to help yourself?**

Viewing reality as static provides a false perspective of reality,

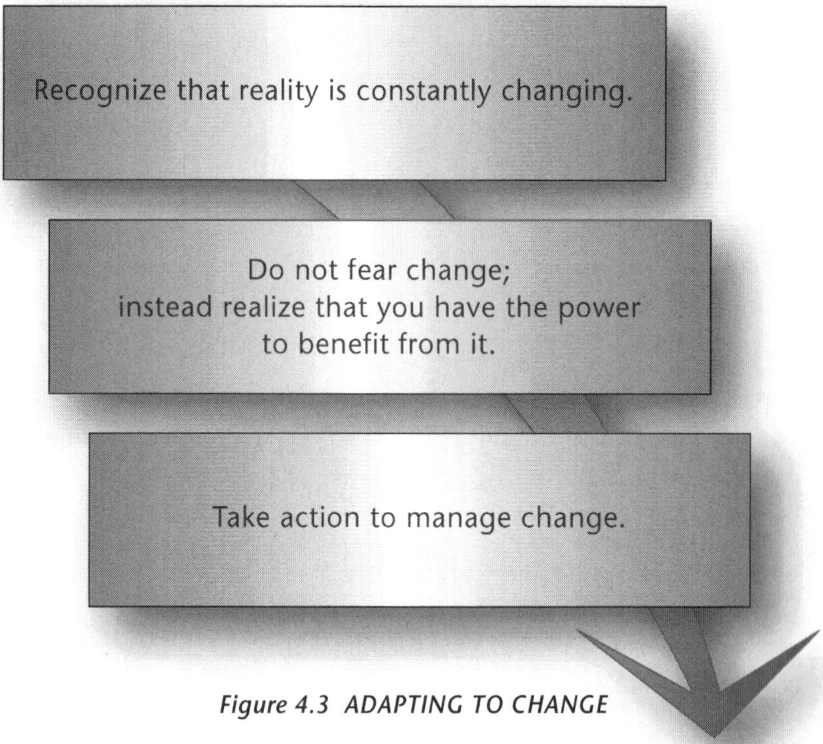

| Recognize that reality is constantly changing. |

| Do not fear change;
instead realize that you have the power
to benefit from it. |

| Take action to manage change. |

Figure 4.3 ADAPTING TO CHANGE

gives you a false sense of security, and conditions you to resist change when it may be in your best interest to adapt to it to improve your life.

2. Why are people more comfortable with a static view of reality?

Because it creates the illusion of stability and security, whereas uncertainty can lead to uneasiness about your safety and peace of mind.

3. Why is it important to accept the dynamic nature of reality?

By doing so, you can be better prepared to adapt to any changes that occur. Facing uncertainty can lead to creativity, possibility, and hope in life.

4. What are some things you can do to accept the dynamic nature of reality?

Clearly perceive and accept the reality of your present circumstances; acknowledge but do not live in the past; accept the inevitability of change and the inherent uncertainty of the future since you cannot control it; set goals and dedicate yourself to accomplishing them.

5. Why are successful people future oriented?

Because they recognize that it doesn't make sense to waste time dwelling on what they cannot change, such as past events or the dynamic nature of reality. They realize that by looking forward and focusing on the factors under their control they can create the future they desire.

Law of Empowerment 4

Nothing can be gained from dwelling on the uncertain nature of reality or focusing on things we cannot change. To shape the future we desire, it is best to accept life with an open mind, prepare to adapt to any change, and focus on factors that are under our control.

Chapter 5

DEVELOPING AND MAINTAINING A MIND OF REINVENTION

Live as if you were to die tomorrow.
Learn as if you were to live forever.

—MAHATMA GANDHI

To find a path to a more successful and happier life, the empowerment mindset requires that we change what we have been doing. However, because the prospect of change brings uncertainty we may remain paralyzed with fear and inaction. To overcome ingrained or learned apprehensions, we need to acquire a powerful desire for transformation and pursue this path with maximum effort, because a weak attempt to create change can result in apathy and resignation. We have to develop a mind of reinvention, one open to accepting new knowledge and willing to adapt to any new situation. Such a mind permits continuous learning, enabling individuals to reinvent themselves at any moment to maintain movement toward beneficial goals.

To further understand what it means to have a mind of reinvention, it is helpful to examine what is meant when referring to the mind. The mind is often associated with the mental processes involved in gaining knowledge and comprehension, including thinking, knowing, remembering, judging, and problem solving. For purposes of our discussion, a useful definition of the mind is: "The human consciousness that originates in the brain and is manifested especially in thought, perception, emotion, will, memory, and imagination."[1]

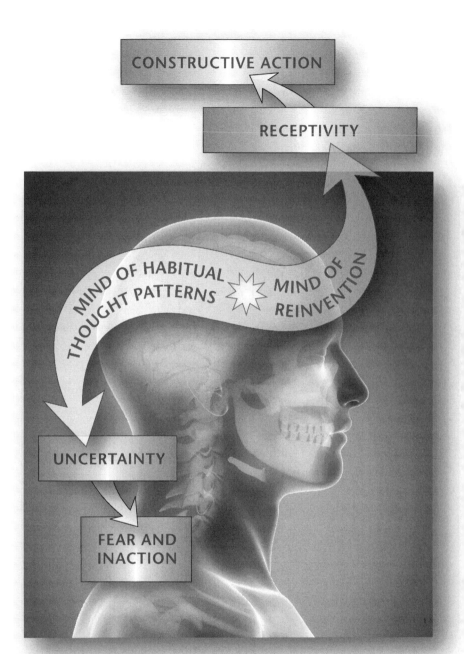

Figure 5.1
USING OUR MIND OF REINVENTION TO KEEP MOVING FORWARD

To have a mind of reinvention means to have a mind receptive to the ideas, attitudes, commitment, and hard work needed to truly improve ourselves and our circumstances. It also means to comprehend that we all have habitual thought patterns harmful to our well-being that automatically determine our responses but which we have the ability to positively change once we become aware of how they reinforce failure and unhappiness. As Ralph Waldo Emerson noted, "The only person you are destined to become is the person you decide to be.[2]

As we have come to understand, habitual thought patterns can be learned from friends or family; acquired from social conditioning, such as from peers or life circumstances; or result from an inflated ego. As infants our minds are completely open, yet we have little control over our bodies. As we age and develop more control over our bodies, our minds often become filled with habitual thought patterns and closed to new ideas that might bring beneficial changes to our lives. Once thought patterns become habitual, they occur subconsciously and negatively color our perceptions, often causing us to become resigned to pessimism and resistant to new and potentially helpful concepts.

At this point, many individuals simply accept the beliefs learned from their parents or life circumstances, resulting in a limited understanding of life and closing their minds to new insights. While people with such self-imposed blinders may believe they are maintaining security and deriving satisfaction from life, they may actually live in a state of continual fear, blame, and regret. They fail to understand that life consists of ever-changing events, with each moment presenting a chance to sample something different or to abandon their comfort zone and relinquish habitual thoughts. However, since people are capable of conscious thought and self-awareness they have the power to determine their responses to situations to create better outcomes.

The importance of having an open mind free of habitual thought patterns is illustrated by the story of a man who visited the house of a famous martial arts master with the hope of becoming his student. After listening for some time to the prospective student chattering nonstop about himself, the master began to pour his tea. The would-be student continued talking but watched nervously as his cup slowly filled and then overflowed, while the master kept pouring. Finally the student blurted out, "Stop, the cup is already full." Slowly the master put the teapot down, stared at him, and said quietly, "Like the cup, your mind is already full. Unless you empty it, there is no room for you to learn." The master instinctually recognized that the student's habitual thought patterns had resulted in a closed mind that was not likely to make him a very good student. To succeed in life and continue growing, we must empty our minds of habitual thoughts, leaving them open to new ideas, opinions, and perspectives. We have to become aware of how the current programming of our attitudes and views might be sabotaging our ability to live happier and more fulfilling lives. To discover how open-minded we are, we could share our views with others in open discussions and observe whether we change our views when evidence shows they are not leading to good results. We regain the openness of mind we possessed as children once we adopt a mind of reinvention.

Yet it is not enough to *achieve* a mind of reinvention; we must also work to *maintain* it. Just as many older people take up forms of exercise such as yoga and tai chi to keep their bodies limber, we must continually exercise our minds so they remain open to new ideas. One way to practice open-mindedness is to evaluate our attitudes and responses when we think we might be dismissing something that could improve our situation, determining whether these attitudes and responses will lead to open-mindedness or keep us stuck in our comfort zone (see figure 5.2). In addition, we can pause every time we hear our inner voice give a typical WSC syndrome response so we gain awareness of how our responses can limit our perspective and have a chance to be more open-minded. For example, if a friend suggests that we do something constructive about a particular problem, instead of listening to our inner voice telling us, "It won't make a difference anyway" or "I am not good enough" or "I can't,"

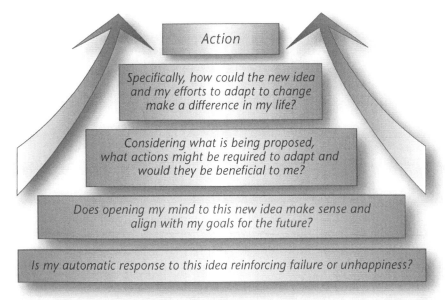

Figure 5.2 PROCESS OF REINVENTION

we can practice having a more open mind by thinking, "Why not give it a try? The least I can do is fail. If I fail, it will not kill me and I will learn something."

At first it might feel uncomfortable to exercise our minds in this way, just as our bodies might experience discomfort when we embark on a new exercise regimen. However, just as our bodies grow stronger and more flexible through continued use so, too, can our minds become stronger and more flexible through practicing having a mind of reinvention.

Key Points

1. **What does having an open mind mean?**

   Understanding that everyone has habitual patterns of thinking that automatically determine their responses and that they possess the ability to positively change these responses once they recognize how they may be leading to failure and unhappiness.

2. What is a mind of reinvention?

A mind open to accepting new knowledge and willing to adapt to new situations. Such a mind permits continuous learning, enabling you to reinvent yourself at any moment to maintain movement toward beneficial goals.

Chapter 6

THE OPEN HEART ATTITUDE

It is only with the heart that one can see rightly; what is essential is invisible to the eye.

—ANTOINE DE SAINT-EXUPERY

To receive the greatest returns in life, the empowerment mindset requires the adoption of an open heart attitude. This is a state of mind that allows individuals to open their hearts to connect deeply to people and to the ocean of life knowledge in a way that permits them to lead more fulfilling lives while protecting themselves from unnecessary hurt and loss of personal power. If the mind provides us with a map to knowledge, the heart is not only our compass but nature's most essential tool for accessing the ocean of life knowledge.

While opening our minds is like learning the words to a song using our intellects, opening our hearts is like learning the music to a song using our innermost feelings. In the words of Helen Keller, "The best and most beautiful things in the world cannot be seen or even touched—they must be felt with the heart."[1] Or as French bishop and theologian Jacques Begigne Bossuel observed, "The heart has reasons that reason does not understand."[2] Further, a Chinese proverb beautifully describes the potential for happiness and fulfillment that having an open heart can create: "[When you] keep a green bough in [your] heart, [a] singing bird will come."[3]

Our hearts are the gateways to our emotions. To open our hearts means to be unafraid to show how we feel, and to be empathetic and receptive to the feelings of others. Conversely, our capacity to empathize with the plight of others is a measure of how open our hearts are. When our hearts are open, we experience the deepest emotions possible—extreme joy and inspiration, as well as profound sadness and despair. What we hold in our hearts is often reflected in our facial expressions and body language, which never lie. For human beings, the deepest feelings of sorrow or happiness find their physical expression in tears. In our Western culture, emotional reserve is often admired while expressing emotions publicly is denigrated as weak. It should be remembered, however, that crying can help lift the emotional burdens we may be carrying.

To open our hearts to others and the cosmos, we need to first open our hearts to ourselves, loving ourselves in a healthy, nonegotistical way. We need to understand that our value lies not in the sum of our material possessions or accomplishments but rather in our intrinsic value as human beings. Authors Gillian Butler, PhD, and Tony Hope advocate valuing ourselves to build our lives on a secure foundation because not doing so undermines our strength and leads to the belief that we are worthless or that our actions are pointless.[4] They further suggest that some of the more common reasons people undervalue themselves include: feeling they are not as important as other people; believing that valuing themselves reflects arrogance; and thinking that valuing themselves shows a lack of moral character.

Since opening our hearts can involve exposing our vulnerabilities to the world, we must do so in a manner that avoids undermining our personal power, which we need to succeed. As Proverbs 4:23 warns, "Above all else, guard your heart, for everything you do flows from it."[5] As a means of guarding their hearts, most people have created levels of trust in various types of relationships. As figure 6.1 shows, people usually place the most trust in their immediate families—their life partners and children—followed by their extended families, close friends, and finally their tribes or communities.

To better understand how cultivating an open heart attitude is important for developing the empowerment mindset, we can think of ourselves as plants growing in the earth's soil. If we are raised in an environment where there is little water or nutrients, our growth will be stunted like small dis-

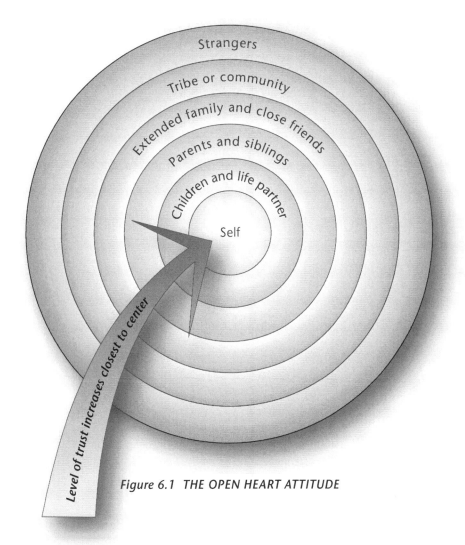

Figure 6.1 *THE OPEN HEART ATTITUDE*

figured trees growing on the rocky shore of some windswept sea. But with sufficient water and nutrients, we will grow tall and strong like a majestic redwood. Similarly, if we live without an open heart attitude we will not receive the emotional nutrients essential for our inner growth, an important element for our eventual success and happiness. Our access to the knowledge of life and the extent of our inner growth are directly related to our cultivation of an open heart attitude.

The Open Heart Attitude

A state of mind that allows individuals to open their hearts to connect deeply to the people in their lives and to the ocean of life knowledge, in a way that permits them to lead more fulfilling and successful lives while protecting themselves from unnecessary hurt and loss of personal power.

Even in this age of narcissism in which people are often focused on vanity, materialism, and the acquisition of power, there are various ways to practice cultivating an open heart attitude. One such practice is prayer, which can be defined as reverent petition to a deity or an object of worship. Whether or not we adhere to an organized religion or spiritual practice, prayers express our innermost thoughts and feelings and thus are a means of opening the heart.

Prayer can have many functions and take numerous forms in various traditions. We pray not only when we make audible petitions but also when we have a prayerful attitude, as American essayist and poet Ralph Waldo Emerson states:

> [Prayer] is not only when we audibly and formally address our petitions to the Deity. We pray without ceasing. *Every secret wish is a prayer. Every desire of the soul and mind is a prayer* uttered to God and registered in heaven. . . . True prayers are the daily, hourly, momentary desires, that enter without impediment, without fear, into the soul.[6] [emphasis added]

In some religions, prayer is a form of communication with nature, the cosmos, or ancestors. Prayer is a fundamental aspect of the spiritual practices of almost every Native American tribe and, as one source notes, "Our religion is not one of paint and feathers; it is a thing of the heart."[7] Members of the Yokut tribe of central California pray, "My words are tied in one with the great mountains, with great rocks, with great trees, in one with my body and heart. All of you see of me, one with this world."[8]

In Christianity the Prayer of the Heart, or the Prayer of Jesus, can be traced back nearly two thousand years to early Christian mysticism and, like many other forms of religious prayer, has specific guidelines.[9] The beautiful prayer of Saint Francis of Assisi reads:

Lord, make me an instrument of your peace
Where there is hatred, let me sow love
Where there is injury, pardon
Where there is doubt, faith
Where there is despair, hope
Where there is darkness, light
Where there is sadness, joy.
O Divine Master,
grant that I may not so much seek to be consoled as to console;
to be understood as to understand;
to be loved as to love.
For it is in giving that we receive
It is in pardoning that we are pardoned
and it is in dying that we are born to eternal life.[10]

For Buddhists, "Prayer is a practice to awaken…inherent inner capacities of strength, compassion and wisdom, rather than to petition external forces based on fear, idolizing, and worldly and/or heavenly gain."[11] To be effective in opening the heart, prayer cannot be used for selfish purposes. As Emerson suggests:

Prayer that craves a particular commodity—anything less than all good—is vicious. Prayer is the contemplation of the facts of life from the highest point of view. It is the soliloquy of a beholding and jubilant soul. It is the spirit of God pronouncing his works good. But prayer as a means to effect a private end is a form of meanness and theft. It supposes dualism and not unity in nature and consciousness. As soon as man is one with God, he will not beg. He will then see prayer in all his actions.[12]

Despite the fact that prayers can be said silently or simply by holding an attitude of reverence, in many traditions prayers are considered stronger when voiced or underscored by actions. For example, according to one source on Sufism, the mystical dimension of Islam, when prayers are said they have more effect, as it is believed that the vibration of sound penetrates the energy centers of the body and reaches the inner plane of our being, producing a greater impact on the soul.[13]

Prayer coupled with movement is even stronger. Movement imprints the thoughts expressed in the prayer on every atom of the body. The whole being, even the atoms and cells, becomes the prayer. "Ask and ye shall receive becomes actualized."[14]

Another technique for opening the heart is to focus on people or matters that have a great impact on our feelings. For example, when I want to get in touch with my deepest feelings I often think of people who mean the most to me but who are no longer here, such as my father, Chief Barry Helin, or favorite uncle, Chief Art Helin, who embodied the open heart attitude and whose warmth, generosity, and good nature lifted the spirits of others like boats in a rising tide. I think about the beautiful emotional and philosophical talks we had that inspired and affected me deeply. I also think about my grandson, Lucius, whose innocence and adventurous spirit remind everyone around him what it is like to have a sparkle in your eye and a bounce in your step. Similarly, I consider the children in the inner city where I teach free martial arts lessons, whose playful natures transmit wonderful energy that dissipates the negative feelings created by their harsh circumstances or stresses of everyday existence. In addition, I often think of the gifts I have been given throughout my life in the form of family and friends, and how having been born at this time and in this place is like winning the cosmic lottery. As well, I compare my life circumstances to the grueling treadmill of poverty and despair endured by people who must suffer the tragic fate of seeing their families torn apart by situations they cannot control. Such thoughts can open our hearts and, by extension, the hearts of others.

Spirit Lifters at Work

Above left, the author's father, Sm'ooygit Nees Nuugan Noos (Chief Barry Helin); above right, the author's uncle, Sm'ooygit Hyemass (Chief Art Helin).

Yet another way of opening the heart that has been recognized by people throughout civilization is through music—either by playing a musical instrument, singing, chanting, or listening to music. Although listening to music can evoke emotional responses, actively creating music is generally a more effective way of opening the heart. Participating in other art forms, such as dance or writing poetry, can have a similarly beneficial impact on our hearts.

Throughout history, indigenous peoples have developed various ways of opening the heart and creating a sense of spiritual community through music and all other art forms, including drumming, chanting, and community dancing. Other spiritual practices include rituals, prayers, and incantations that create a sense of spiritual community and open people's hearts through shared experiences.

Whether we open our hearts through spiritual practices, focus on people or matters that have greatly impacted our feelings, or participate in music or other art forms is not important. The goal—cultivating an open heart attitude to provide a valuable tool for learning and experiencing the most fulfilling life possible—is what matters. We need to lovingly nurture ourselves and develop an open heart attitude so we can become giant human redwoods, living life to its fullest and sharing our bounty with others.

Key Points

1. Why is cultivating an open heart attitude important?

   The heart is the source of the most profound emotional experiences and the greatest nourishment of the human psyche. Cultivating an open heart attitude allows you to connect to others in meaningful ways and is the most valuable tool you can possess for learning and for experiencing the most fulfilling life possible.

2. What are some ways to practice cultivating an open heart attitude?

   Through prayer or other spiritual practices; by focusing on people or matters that have greatly impacted your feelings; and through music or other art forms.

Chapter 7

GROWING BY GIVING

*I have found that among its other benefits,
giving liberates the soul of the giver.*

—MAYA ANGELOU

In our present society, which is dominated by personal consumption and self-absorption, many of us respond to circumstances by wondering how they will benefit us, thinking what's in it for me? But to adopt and maintain the empowerment mindset we must also understand the benefits of giving. Let me share an example of how shifting my focus from taking to giving both liberated me and created a larger context for my own personal agenda.

At one point in my career as a young attorney, I became increasingly focused on chasing money. As I did this to the exclusion of more significant aspects of my life, the support I received from others and the opportunities that came my way completely disappeared. Eventually spiraling toward bankruptcy, I questioned but did not understand the deeper reasons for this. Like the *Titanic*, my ship was going down, and swapping deck chairs in my mind was making no difference to my impending fate. Finally I started to think about the advice my father had given me when I was growing up: "Just do the right thing, and everything else will follow." I then remembered why my father and grandmother had sent me, as a twelve-year-old, over five-hundred miles from our remote Native American community to a large city to get an education—to help indigenous and other disadvantaged or suffering people find a better way of life.

One night in the midst of my confusion I was awakened by a dream in which a gigantic raven flew into a house, landed at the end of a room where I was speaking to a group of people in a condescending manner, and chided me for my terrible attitude and manners. Since the raven was the primary crest and guardian spirit of the tribe in which my grandmother was chieftain, I interpreted the dream as my grandmother wanting me to dedicate my efforts to seeking genuine solutions and to become a soldier in the effort to provide hope to the generations of lost indigenous people suffering from persecution or disadvantage. This dream helped me formulate a life's purpose that involved giving to others and not simply taking for myself.

As a result of this shift in focus, I began to change in surprising ways. Giving and being empathetic allowed me to genuinely connect with people and garner others' support for my efforts because they respected my life's purpose. Also I began to notice how giving to others with no expectation of receiving anything in return brought unforeseen gifts that previously would have been impossible for me to imagine, providing me with a sense of fulfillment that was wonderful compensation—a phenomenon I called the law of giving.

I now understood that, as a hereditary chief of a Native American tribe, my father had practiced this kind of giving all his life, for which he was compensated with great respect and the status of chief. And I became more aware of the benefits of a ritualized form of giving practiced by indigenous people of the northwest coast of Canada, known as the "potlatch," which is both a way for people to demonstrate their wealth, generosity, status, and power, and a ritual that confers specific powers on the givers while ensuring distribution of material wealth to all tribal members. Further, I learned that my father's advice was similar to the ideas of American philosopher Ralph Waldo Emerson, who observed, "It is one of the most beautiful compensations of this life that no one can sincerely try to help another without helping himself."[1] Emerson further explained that there is:

> a dualism [that] underlies the nature and condition of man. Every excess causes a defect; every defect an excess. Every sweet hath its sour; every evil its good.…Give and it shall be given you. He that watereth shall be watered himself.… Love and you shall be loved.… *The good man has absolute good, which like fire turns everything to its own nature, so that you cannot do him any harm…*[2] [emphasis added]

Another personal example of the compensation derived from giving is an event that took place over ten years ago when I asked my karate teacher, Sensei Toshiaki Nomada, to become the head instructor of a martial arts club I wanted to establish to offer free martial arts lessons to impoverished inner-city children. Even though Sensei Nomada was in superb physical condition, he was seriously hindered by poor eyesight, which prevented him from working. However, in an environment where the light was fixed, such as the one I had in mind, he could see well enough to teach karate. Our idea was to provide a structured environment where kids could learn to focus and develop discipline, manners, and respect—valuable skills they could apply in other aspects of their lives, such as acquiring a good education and securing employment.

At first people thanked us for giving our time, resources, and expertise to the children. After several months, however, Sensei Nomada said he wanted to thank me for helping to set up the club. Sensing my surprise, he explained that because of his eyesight he couldn't work, and so he appreciated the opportunity to be involved in an activity where he could receive the "beautiful energy" that the children provided. Thus the enterprise compensated us both in ways neither of us could have imagined.

The idea of compensation is reflected in a more cosmic sense in the concept of karma, a Sanskrit word that refers to our motivations while performing actions and how whatever we do intentionally to others we experience ourselves in some similar way in the future.[3] However, even the concept of karma recognizes that we have the power to shape our future, as explained by the His Holiness the 14th Dalai Lama of Tibet, who observed:

> Some people misunderstand the concept of karma. They take the Buddha's doctrine of the law of causality to mean that all is predetermined, that there is nothing that the individual can do. This is a total misunderstanding. The very term karma or action is a term of active force, which indicates that *future events are within your own hands*. Since action is a phenomenon that is committed by a person, a living being, *it is within your own hands whether or not you engage in action*.[4] [emphasis added]

A powerful image of how people are compensated when they help others occurs in a Japanese fable recounted by authors Craig and Marc Kielburger in their book *From Me to We: Turning Self-Help on Its Head*. The story depicts hell as a place where there is plenty of food yet people are unable to feed themselves. Because they have been given very long chopsticks, the food they pick up cannot reach their mouths, and, as a result, they starve. Heaven, on the other hand, is portrayed as a place that features identical circumstances but people are able to eat because they use their chopsticks to feed one another. The authors write, "Throughout the world there are places where a strong sense of community and reciprocity still survive. There are cultures that have not forgotten that in our most natural state—away from cars and one-bedroom condos and the glare of the television screen—human beings are social creatures who need each other to reach their highest potential."[5]

Giving from our hearts without expecting anything in return allows us to receive more riches than can ever be measured in monetary terms. If we do not have the financial resources to give money, the most important gifts we can give are our knowledge, time, and emotional support. This type of giving helps us adopt and maintain the empowerment mindset, which allows us to achieve greater personal success and happiness.

Key Points

1. **What is the law of giving?**

   Giving with no expectation of receiving anything in return, so the giving is its own reward, compensating the giver with a sense of fulfillment.

2. **Why is it important to give with no expectation of receiving anything in return?**

   Because nature compensates you for everything you do. When you do bad things, you will experience misfortune; and when you give sincerely with your heart, expecting nothing in return, it not only helps others but also confers powers on you for your future growth.

Chapter 8

UNDERSTANDING
THE CONSCIOUS AND
SUBCONSCIOUS MINDS

The potential of the average person is a huge ocean unsailed,
a new continent unexplored,
a world of possibilities waiting to be released and channeled
toward some great good.

—BRIAN TRACY

To unlock our empowerment potential, we need to understand how the conscious and subconscious minds operate and how we can use our conscious minds to program our subconscious minds for helping us succeed in life. Comprehending that our conscious minds can effectively program our subconscious minds through focused visualization to accomplish goals and achieve success is an essential aspect of the empowerment mindset.

RELATIONSHIP BETWEEN THE CONSCIOUS AND
THE SUBCONSCIOUS MIND

Whatever we plant in our subconscious mind and nourish with repetition and emotion will one day become a reality.

—EARL NIGHTINGALE

The conscious mind is objective and discriminating, looking at the world rationally and with clarity. It perceives surroundings, sensations, and thoughts; interprets physical data through the senses of sight, hearing, smell, taste, and touch; and allows us to take action. It is the originator of thought and, through intentional programming, can empower the subconscious mind to achieve the goals we set. As a result of this command position, it is referred to as the "executive control room of the mind."[1]

Merriam-Webster's Collegiate Dictionary defines the subconscious mind as "existing in the mind but not immediately available to consciousness."[2] The subconscious mind can be further defined as psychic activity below the level of awareness. Such psychic activity can include unconscious feelings, thoughts, habits, automatic skills, reactions, complexes, unnoticed

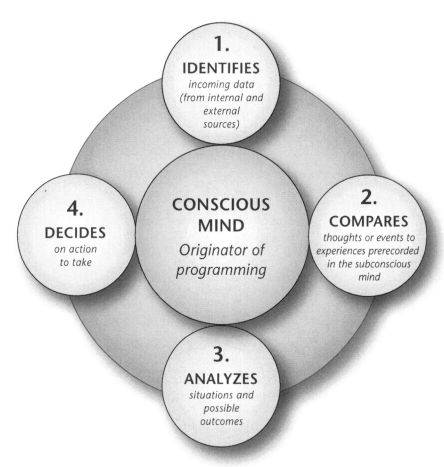

Figure 8.1 THE CONSCIOUS MIND

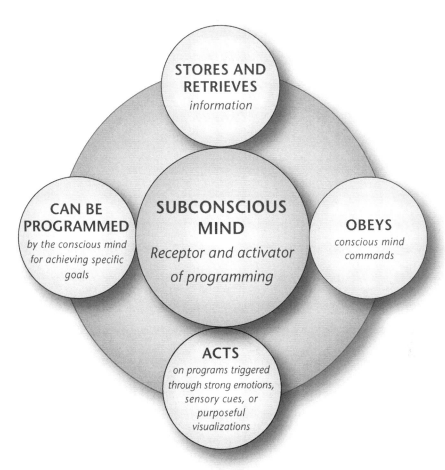

Figure 8.2 THE SUBCONSCIOUS MIND

perceptions, hidden phobias, and concealed desires.[3] When danger arises, the subconscious mind is responsible for the fight-or-flight response. It has memory but no original thoughts. Operating much faster than the conscious mind, it is a powerful databank that stores and retrieves subjective information. The conscious mind is said to be responsible for perhaps 10 percent of the activity of the mind, and the subconscious mind for the remaining 90 percent.

The term "subconscious mind" is often avoided in academic or scientific circles, or relegated to the realm of "pop psychology," because neuroscience has yet to demonstrate its existence. Yet one source explains that "researchers at Columbia University Medical Center have discovered that fleeting images of fearful faces—images that appear and disappear so quickly that they escape conscious awareness—produce unconscious anxiety that can be detected in the brain with the latest neuroimaging machines and that the conscious mind is hundreds of milliseconds behind those unconscious processes."[4] Consequently, the fact that there is no certain scientific verification of the existence of the subconscious mind may simply mean science is either unable at present to provide it or that the activity of the subconscious mind is not measurable in scientific terms but can still affect people, somewhat like the psychic concept of chi believed to exist in Chinese culture.

While people make rational choices with their conscious minds, their subconscious minds make unconscious choices that can activate preprogrammed commands. In discussing how sensory cues can cause the subconscious mind to act on a program, a *New York Times* article discloses how "priming" people through sensory cues using everyday sights, smells, and sounds can cause people to selectively pursue goals that they already have.[5] In other words, the subconscious mind is far more active and independent than was previously known, and "neural software programs" can be employed purposely to achieve goals. Thus if we are trying to escape the WSC syndrome, achieve goals, or lead more fulfilling lives there is great value in understanding how the subconscious mind can generate better outcomes.

In trying to understand how the conscious and subconscious minds work, it may be useful to think in terms of a computer. In such an analogy, the conscious mind is like the computer's central processing unit (CPU) and the peripherals, such as keyboard, camera, and audio mike, work together to process inputted data. The subconscious mind is much like the hard drive that stores data from previous CPU inputs. However, the subconscious mind operates somewhat differently from a hard drive in that it can send instructions back out to create reactions in situations where external cues have bypassed the conscious mind. Such cues can automatically activate the pre-programmed software specific to the individual. Alternatively, the person, upon receiving the sensory input, can make a conscious decision to either take action or program the subconscious mind for success. Consequently, although the two minds have separate functions, they operate in synchronization, as shown in figure 8.3.

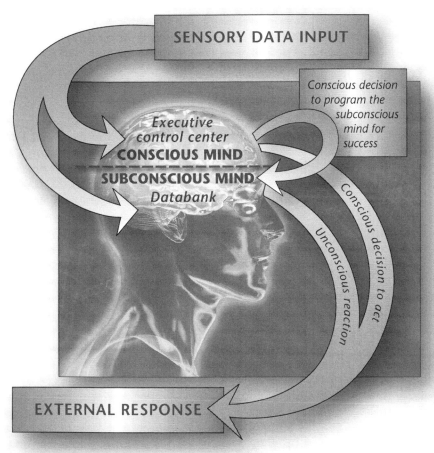

Figure 8.3
SYNCHRONIZATION OF THE CONSCIOUS AND SUBCONSCIOUS MINDS

PROGRAMMING
THE SUBCONSCIOUS MIND FOR SUCCESS

*The conscious mind may be compared to a fountain
playing in the sun and falling back into the great subterranean pool
of subconscious from which it rises.*

—SIGMUND FREUD

There are several steps in programming the subconscious mind to help us achieve success and unlock our empowerment potential. These are (1) visualization; (2) commitment and reinforcement; (3) emotionaliza-

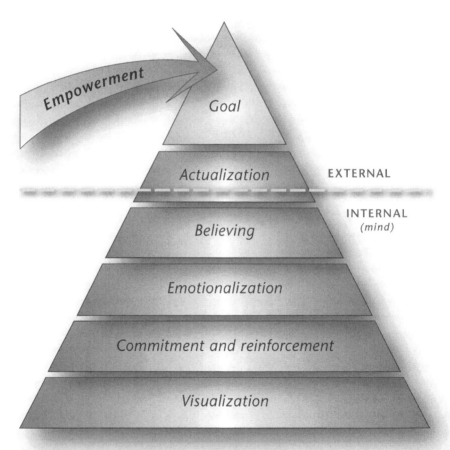

Figure 8.4 *PROGRAMMING THE SUBCONSCIOUS MIND FOR SUCCESS*

tion; (4) believing; and (5) actualization. Let us now examine how each of these steps can help us adopt the empowerment mindset and move forward in our lives.

1. Visualization

I've discovered that numerous peak performers use the skill of mental rehearsal of visualization.
They mentally run through important events before they happen.

—CHARLES A. GARFIELD

The first step in programming the subconscious mind is visualization. The most immediate and lasting impressions, particularly in the subconscious mind, are visual images. Leading communications expert Professor Albert Mehrabian has scientifically measured the impact that verbal, vocal, and visual impressions have on audiences. Concluding that visual impressions have a much greater impact than verbal or vocal ones, Mehrabian states:

◆ Verbal impressions (the actual words spoken) account for only 7 percent of the impact.

◆ Vocal impressions (tone, range, appeal, and "credibility" of the speaker's voice) account for 38 percent of the impact.

◆ Visual impressions (the speaker's physical appearance, clothing, gestures, stance, eye contact, and more) account for 55 percent of the impact.[6]

This phenomenon explains why there was a difference of opinion between radio listeners and television viewers about who won the first televised presidential debates between Richard Nixon and John Kennedy. Radio listeners, who only heard the debates, thought Richard Nixon had won, while television viewers, who saw the debates, thought John Kennedy had triumphed.[7]

Visual impressions are immediate and powerful. They flow instantaneously into our subconscious minds, whereas words must first be processed in our conscious minds into sentences and thoughts, which may or may not eventually evoke visual impressions. Jack Canfield states, "Your creative subconscious doesn't think in words—it can only think in pictures."[8] Therefore, if we want to harness the power of our subconscious minds we can do so by visualizing precisely what it is we wish to accomplish.[9]

Visualization is a powerful way to effect change because our subconscious minds are like graphic processors that imprint detailed images and their perceived meaning instantly and directly onto our emotions and psyches. The subconscious mind works like a profiler seeking to match all sensory input with what is stored in its database. Canfield states that visualization is one of our most underutilized tools for accelerating success by:

◆ Activating the powers of our subconscious minds by creating solutions for accomplishing our goals.

◆ Focusing the reticular cortex (the part of the brain relevant to awareness) by programming its reticular activating system (RAS) to become aware of previously available but unnoticed and untapped resources.[10] The RAS operates like a telephone switchboard so that when we visualize a goal our reticular cortex makes us aware of available people, information, and opportunities that can help us achieve the goal.[11]

◆ Creating a new level of motivation by attracting people, resources, and opportunities needed to achieve our goals.[12]

Further, Canfield reports how Harvard researchers found that students who visualized in advance performed tasks with nearly 100 percent accuracy, compared to 55 percent accuracy for those who didn't visualize.[13]

Similarly, athletes find it useful to visualize techniques to assist in performing them correctly. Athletes can utilize visualization to either manifest the intention of an outcome of a competition or training session or create a feeling of calm and well-being.[14]

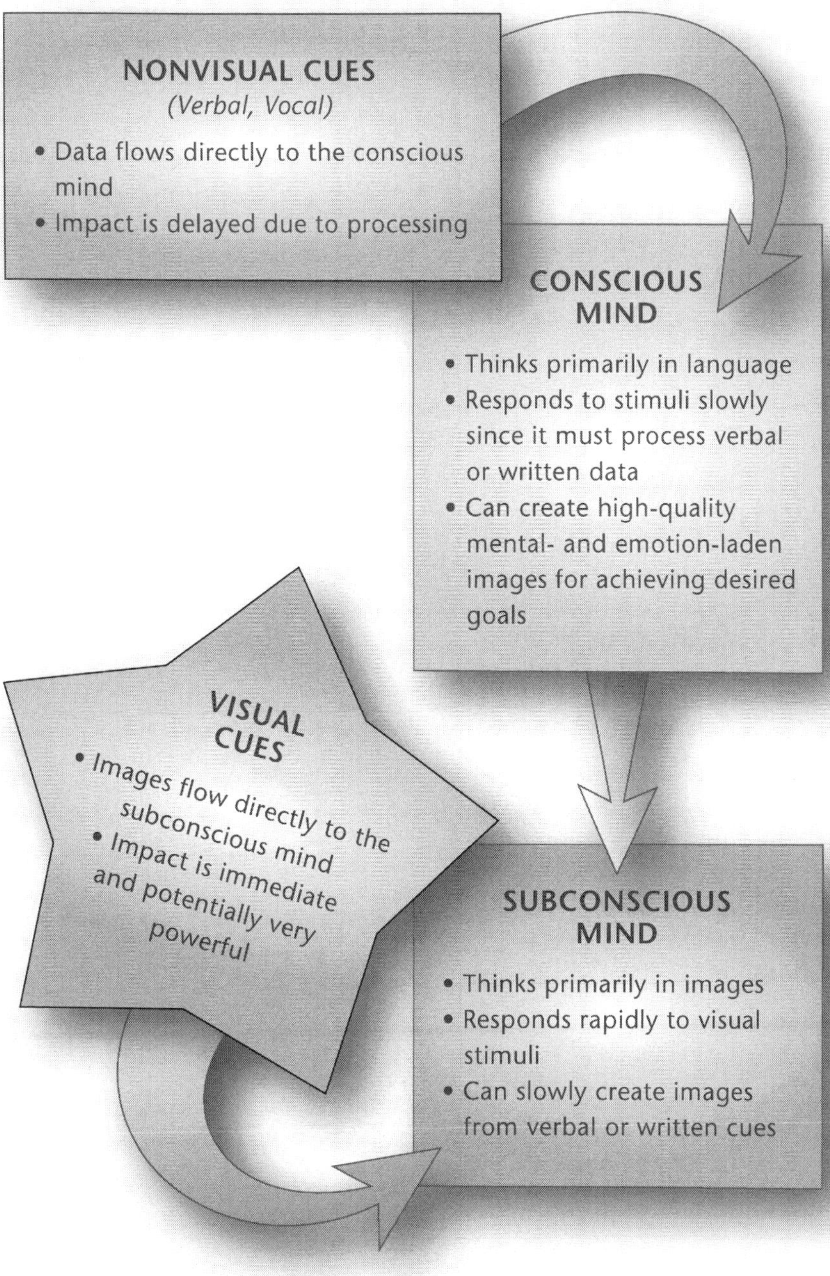

NONVISUAL CUES
(Verbal, Vocal)

• Data flows directly to the conscious mind
• Impact is delayed due to processing

CONSCIOUS MIND

• Thinks primarily in language
• Responds to stimuli slowly since it must process verbal or written data
• Can create high-quality mental- and emotion-laden images for achieving desired goals

VISUAL CUES

• Images flow directly to the subconscious mind
• Impact is immediate and potentially very powerful

SUBCONSCIOUS MIND

• Thinks primarily in images
• Responds rapidly to visual stimuli
• Can slowly create images from verbal or written cues

Figure 8.5 FLOW OF INFORMATION TO THE SUBCONSCIOUS MIND

Legendary golfer Jack Nicklaus explains his technique for visualizing in the following way:

> I never hit a shot, not even in practice, without having a very sharp, in-focus picture of it in my head. It's like a color movie. First I "see" where I want it to finish, nice and white and sitting high on the bright green grass. The scene quickly changes, and I see the ball going there: its path, trajectory, and shape, even its behavior on landing. Then there's a sort of a fade-out, and the next scene shows me making the kind of swing that will turn the previous images into reality.[15]

As a karate instructor who has studied this martial art for over thirty years, I also learned that when you demonstrate a technique rather than talk about it, students learn much faster. Seeing a technique done properly allows them to duplicate the picture that has gone into their subconscious minds, as opposed to generating the picture after hearing a verbal description of it.

People who want to unlock their empowerment potential to achieve success and happiness can use visualization in a variety of ways. First, visualization is helpful as a mental rehearsal to ensure we are familiar with and relaxed about an upcoming event important for reaching one of our goals. Second, using visualization to picture achieving a goal conditions our brains to believe that attaining it is possible. Third, visualization enables us to realize a goal sooner since creating a mental image of a goal attracts the conditions necessary to achieve it.

Visualizing the goals we want to reach and the outcomes we would like to see in our lives is critical to attaining them. If we are not clear about what we want to achieve, we will most likely never succeed. To clarify goals so that we can program our subconscious minds effectively, we have to reflect on them deeply and articulate them specifically by writing them down, thereby reinforcing them and reminding us to make choices that will lead to their accomplishment. It may be useful to initially visualize a relatively easy goal that we believe we can achieve in a timely manner and then work up to more difficult ones.

Once we have clarified a goal, the most powerful way to program our subconscious minds to help us achieve it is to send it clear, detailed pictures of what we want, visualizing the goal as if it has already been accomplished, perhaps drawing a picture of the goal for even greater clarity. In doing this, as seen in Nicklaus's visualization technique, we should break a goal down into a series of individual images corresponding to steps needed to reach the goal to let the subconscious mind know what is required to complete the process.

This technique helps define our desires and provides the conscious mind with a very clear picture to imbed in the subconscious mind. Once the subconscious mind sees what we want, it will help us make our desires a reality.

2. Commitment and Reinforcement

It was character that got us out of bed,
commitment that moved us into action,
and discipline that enabled us to follow through.

—ZIG ZIGLAR

The second step in programming the subconscious mind to help us achieve success and unlock our empowerment potential is to have commitment to a goal and then periodically reinforce that commitment until we achieve the goal. Committing to a goal focuses our energy more strongly than simply having an interest in a goal. When we are interested in doing something, we do it only if circumstances are favorable. When we commit to accomplishing something, however, we do it regardless of the circumstances or create the circumstances necessary to do it. To commit to something, we have to make a solemn promise to ourselves, such as, "Come hell or high water I am going to do X." In a sense, this gives us "skin in the game" so we feel we have something to lose if we do not perform.

After committing to a goal, it is important to continually reinforce the commitment. We do this first by reviewing its details and importance. Then we write a positive affirmation concerning the goal. For example, "My goal is to earn $50,000 by December 31, 20xx by tapping into my reserves of talent and drive." Finally, we establish a daily routine of looking at the written affirmation and repeating it at certain times of the day, such as when getting out of bed, before coffee breaks and meals, and prior to going to bed, until we achieve the goal. Adhering to this process plants the goal firmly in our subconscious minds and serves to further unlock our empowerment potential.

3. Emotionalization

All thoughts which have been emotionalized (given feeling)
and mixed with faith begin immediately to translate themselves
into their physical equivalents or counterparts.

—NAPOLEON HILL

The third step in programming the subconscious mind to help us achieve success and unlock our empowerment potential is emotionalization. Emotionalization combines imagining a goal with the most positive feelings that foster its realization. According to the law of attraction, the more positively emotionalized thoughts about goals are the more they will attract what we seek. Author and pioneer of personal-success literature Napoleon Hill suggested that thoughts mixed with emotion magnetically attract other similar or related thoughts.[16]

To emotionalize thoughts about goals, first we must think about how achieving a particular goal would impact our feelings. For example, if we want to earn more money we might imagine how euphoric we would feel having accomplished a goal that would permit us to spend more time with our family, provide our children with more opportunities, and earn us the admiration of our spouse. We can think as well about the confidence it would give us to take on other challenges, how good it would feel to succeed at something important, and how liberated we would be to move forward in our lives.

4. Believing

Your beliefs become your thoughts. Your thoughts become your words.
Your words become your actions. Your actions become your habits. Your
habits become your values. Your values become your destiny.

—MAHATMA GANDHI

The fourth step in programming the subconscious mind to help us achieve success and unlock our empowerment potential is believing. Believing, which has been defined as a state of mind in which trust or confidence is placed in some person or thing,[17] functions somewhat like commitment to program our subconscious minds to help us achieve goals. Believing strongly in our ability to achieve a particular goal removes doubt and ensures that we generate positive energy concerning it, as opposed to lacking faith in our ability to achieve our goal and generating negative energy around it. According to one source, when we ultimately reach a goal we should acknowledge that we made it happen and give ourselves "a pat on the back"[18] to further reinforce the power of our subconscious minds to achieve future goals.

5. Actualization

I think there is something more important than believing: Action!
The world is full of dreamers; there aren't enough who will move ahead
and begin to take concrete steps to actualize their vision.

—W. CLEMENT STONE

The fifth step in programming the subconscious mind to help us achieve success and unlock our empowerment potential is actualization. To actualize means to turn into action.[19] For purposes of our discussion, actualization means two things. First, actualization means thinking and behaving as if we have already accomplished our goal since, according to the law of attraction, when we do this people and circumstances align for us to achieve it. Second, actualization means taking action after using our conscious minds to program our subconscious minds. Although visualization of a goal is important to produce change, clear mental images have to be followed with purposeful action to assure success.

We have now come to understand the significant relationship between the conscious and the subconscious minds, and how intentional programming of our subconscious minds can empower us to achieve the goals we set

Figure 8.6
PROGRAMMING THE SUBCONSCIOUS MIND TO HELP ACHIEVE GOALS

for ourselves. In examining the five steps of visualization, commitment and reinforcement, emotionalization, believing, and actualization, we have learned how we unlock our empowerment potential to achieve greater success and fulfillment.

Key Points

1. What is the conscious mind?

It is the rational part of the mind that originates thought; interprets physical data through the senses of sight, hearing, smell, taste, and touch; and allows us to take deliberate action.

2. What is the subconscious mind?

It is the part of the mind that involves psychic activity below the level of awareness, such as unconscious feelings, thoughts, habits, automatic skills, reactions, complexes, unnoticed perceptions, hidden phobias, and concealed desires. It is a massive databank that stores and retrieves subjective information. It operates much faster than the conscious mind and is responsible for most of the mind's activity.

3. What is the relationship between the conscious and subconscious minds?

They operate in synchronization. Your conscious mind can purposely program your subconscious mind to help you achieve your goals.

4. What steps are involved in programming the subconscious mind?

Visualization, commitment and reinforcement, emotionalization, believing, and actualization.

Law of Empowerment 5

Our conscious minds can purposely program our subconscious minds to help us reach our goals through visualization, commitment and reinforcement, emotionalization, believing, and actualization.

Chapter 9

THE POWER OF
THE HUMAN SPIRIT

And men go forth to wonder at the heights of mountains.
The huge waves of the sea,
The broad flow of the rivers,
The extent of the ocean,
The courses of the stars,
And omit to wonder at themselves.

—**SAINT AUGUSTINE**

To cultivate an empowerment mindset that will allow us to accomplish our goals, we need to unleash the potential power of perhaps our greatest unused asset—the human spirit. We can do this by becoming spiritual warriors.

According to one source, the word *spirit* is derived from the Latin *spiritus*, which literally means "breath."[1] Another definition of the human spirit is "the soul, considered as departing from the body."[2] The human spirit has further been defined as "the animating, sensitive or vital principle in [the] individual, similar to the soul taken to be the seat of the mental, intellectual and emotional powers."[3] The notions of a person's spirit and soul often overlap. While some people believe there is no such thing as a soul, that an individual ceases to exist at the moment of death, in many religious, spiritual, and philosophical traditions the soul or spirit is thought to be the nonphysical, eternal essence of a person that leaves the body when that person dies. For example, the Bible states: "And fear not them which kill the body, but are not able to kill the soul: but rather fear Him which is able to destroy both soul and body in hell."[4] According to some religions, God creates souls. Other groups, particularly indigenous ones, believe all living things—even inanimate objects such as rocks—have souls or spirits, a belief known as animism.[5]

A central belief in some religions and spiritual traditions, such as Hinduism, Jainism, Sikhism, and Buddhism, is reincarnation—a cycle of rebirths in which one's consciousness moves from life to life. References to this idea are also found in Taoism, as stated by fourth-century BCE philosopher Chuang Tzu:

> Birth is not a beginning; death is not an end. There is existence without limitation; there is continuity without a starting-point. Existence without limitation is Space. Continuity without a starting point is Time. There is birth, there is death, there is issuing forth, there is entering in.[6]

My Native American Tsimshian tribe of the northwest coast of Canada believes in reincarnation and even has a word, *baa'lx*, used to identify a child born with characteristics that resemble those of a deceased person. For example, I have a four-year-old great-nephew we call Little Ol' Joe who acts in some ways like an old man, such as being patient when performing certain tasks, leading tribal elders to say he is the *baa'lx* of some previously living person.

Little Ol' Joe

In addition to these beliefs in the existence of the human spirit, many prominent authors have acknowledged the potential of the human spirit as a valuable resource for success. For example, German physician and chemist Philius A. Paracelsus said, "Man never made any material as resilient as the human spirit."[7] Former Vice President Hubert Humphrey commented, "There are incalculable resources in the human spirit once it has been set free."[8] Visionary storyteller Joseph Fabry said, "The human spirit is your specifically human dimension and contains abilities other creatures do not have. Every human is spiritual; in fact, spirit is the essence of being human. You have a body that may become ill; you have a psyche that may become disturbed. But the spirit is what you are. It is your healthy core."[9]

An example of the power and triumph of the human spirit can be seen in the story of a young Native American named Dave Tuccaro Jr. On December 23, 2006, Dave was launched on an unexpected journey that would lead him to understand and appreciate the profound gift that life truly is. On that day at 10:00 p.m., he was taken to a local hospital complaining of low energy and poor vision, symptoms he thought were the result of a bad case of the flu. On Christmas Eve, he was emergency airlifted to a major hospital, where he was diagnosed with acute lymphoblastic leukemia (ALL)—a type of cancer of the blood and bone marrow—which led to a five-year odyssey requiring him to fight tooth and nail for his life.

Dave's struggle to live required him to endure eight hip biopsies, two rounds of intense chemotherapy, six rounds of full body radiation, an addiction to painkillers, an epidural (a form of analgesia involving an injection into the spine), a bone marrow transplant, a disease called graph-versus-host (GVHD—when cells from the transplanted tissue of a donor initiate an immunologic attack on the cells and tissue of the recipient), avascular necrosis (deterioration of bone due to diminished blood supply), and kidney disease (caused by medication).

Had Dave's battle to live ended here, it would have been nothing short of incredible. However, even more challenges were in store for him. His treatment necessitated high doses of prednisone (a synthetic steroid similar to cortisone used as an antiallergic, immunosuppressive, and anticancer drug), which resulted in essentially destroying all his major joints. To date, Dave has had two hips and one shoulder joint replaced, and will soon need the other shoulder joint replaced as well as knee, ankle, and elbow joints. Now living in Los Angeles, he recently met with Christian Holtmann, the man from Germany who donated the bone marrow that saved his life, to express his gratitude. Despite Dave's horrendous ordeal, he has maintained his sense of humor, using his love of music to pull him through the darkest times, thus earning the moniker DJ Bionic Dave. Dave Tuccaro Jr. is a true spiritual warrior, an example of someone who has had to tap into immense spiritual resources to endure a battle for survival.

While Dave's journey is exceptional and not one most of us will be called upon to take, we, too, can tap into our spiritual resources to help us on our life paths. To access our spiritual resources and become spiritual warriors like Dave Tuccaro Jr., we need to cultivate the kind of courage that is often referred to as "martial spirit," or in Japanese 闘志, literally

Demons of Pain

"fighting spirit"—the quality a warrior, soldier, athlete, or fighter must possess to be successful.[10] While we may never be called upon to serve in battle or face an opposing team, we must develop our power as spiritual warriors to face challenges that prevent us from realizing our true potential. Unless we approach challenges with the passionate dedication characteristic of spiritual warriors, we risk falling to the opposing forces of negative emotions, toxic thoughts, or other self-sabotaging habits that may stand in the way of our success. As novelist and screenwriter David Ambrose once said, "If you have the will to win, you have achieved half your success; if you don't, you have achieved half your failure."[11] Tapping into the power of perhaps our greatest asset—our human spirit—we can call upon it to support us in all our endeavors, including that of cultivating an empowerment mindset.

Key Points

1. What is the human spirit?

   It is the nonphysical animating force that is considered the seat of all mental, intellectual, and emotional powers.

2. Why is it important?

   It is the source of our greatest resiliency and courage and thus can help us succeed in all our endeavors, including cultivating an empowerment mindset.

Law of Empowerment 6

To succeed, we need to draw on the resources of our hearts and spirits, so that we are always open to learning, are prepared to adapt to any new situation, and have the courage to take positive and decisive action.

Chapter 10

FEAR, FAILURE, AND RISK

Success consists in going from failure to failure with enthusiasm.

—WINSTON CHURCHILL

Many people become imprisoned by an unwillingness to take risks due to fear of failure. Or they become so habituated to failure that they give up trying to improve their lives and settle for a false sense of security. But to be successful in life we have to face our fears, the possibility of failure, and accept the necessity of taking risks. Author A. P. Gouthey pragmatically noted that it is impossible to get profit without risk, or experience without danger, or reward without work.[1] Motivational speaker and author Denis Waitley further advised that failure should be our teacher not our undertaker—delaying our journey but not preventing us from reaching our destiny.[2]

Fear can often be damaging, regardless of any decision to act, since the anxiety, stress, and unhappiness resulting from fear cause perhaps more harm than the reality of what we fear. Former President Franklin D. Roosevelt famously noted the harmful effects of fear when he said in his First Inaugural Address, "The only thing we have to fear is fear itself."[3] Because the law of attraction also operates for negative forces, which work like prayers in reverse, attracting destructive rather than constructive elements, fearing something attracts what we fear and is more likely to lead to harm—like when the proverbial dog bites the most fearful person in a group. But many people living in constant fear are often unaware of or unwilling to admit its damaging impact on their lives.

Fear can also be damaging because various fears reinforce one another. Napoleon Hill contended that there are seven major fears that reinforce each other—fear of poverty, criticism, ill health, loss of love, loss of liberty, old age, and death.[4] To this list I would add the fear of failure and risk.

However, as Hill suggested, although fear can steal our peace of mind and people who achieve success are not immune to fear, such individuals know how to avoid the negative emotions that fear can stir up, such as anger and jealousy, instead focusing on constructive influences that bring empowerment.[5]

Dale Carnegie pointed out that all life is a risk, and those who accomplish the most are the ones willing to take risks.[6] Indeed, as American theater critic Brooks Atkinson notes, America "was built by men who took risks—pioneers who were not afraid of the wilderness, businessmen who were not afraid of failure, scientists who were not afraid of the truth, thinkers who were not afraid of progress, dreamers who were not afraid of action."[7] By not taking risks necessary to abandon habitual failure and set goals for success, it is guaranteed that our lives will not get any better. As England's greatest dramatist and poet William Shakespeare noted:

Our doubts are traitors,

And make us lose the good we often might win,

By fearing to attempt.[8]

The first step in dealing with fear is to face it since we cannot transcend what we do not confront. To face our fears about failure, we must become responsible and prepare to deal with each obstacle we encounter. Nathaniel Branden suggests a path that involves being proactive; focused and purposeful; responsible for every choice, decision, and action; fully accountable; clear on what is within our power; able to bounce back from defeat to continue moving forward; and able to demonstrate an unmistakable commitment to facing reality.[9] In addition, it may be helpful to ease into changes incrementally, taking small steps at first so that our fear of a big transformation does not prevent us from making constructive changes.

Finally, we must adjust our view of failure, seeing it as a potential learning experience rather reflecting our lack of capabilities. This is especially important because focusing on past failure attracts future failure. Failure should be seen simply as part of the learning process necessary to succeed. While it is critical to learn lessons from our failures, we must do so with an attitude reflecting our preparedness to move forward and follow our life's purpose. The danger of not having such an attitude is reflected in a survey of over thirty thousand people showing that it had taken only one setback to cause many to accept lifelong defeat.[10] Personal-success writer Napoleon Hill

1 Face fear.
We cannot transcend what we do not confront.

2 Prepare to deal with adversity.
Overcoming adversity involves being proactive, focused, purposeful, and accountable; clear about what is within our power; resilient in the face of defeat; and committed to facing reality

3 Do not dwell on past failure.
Focusing on past failure attracts future failure.

4 Learn from failure.
Lessons learned from failure move us beyond defeat.

5 Adopt a constructive attitude toward failure.
Finding value in failure accelerates our momentum along the path to success.

Figure 10.1 STEPS TO OVERCOMING FEARS ABOUT FAILURE

observed that this group had become obsessed with their failure, endlessly reliving the pain it had caused, in contrast to successful people who were focused on the future while their failures remained learning experiences in the past.[11]

The sooner we adopt a constructive attitude toward failure, the faster we can move along the path to success. As former President Franklin D. Roosevelt said, "It is common sense to take a method and try it. If it fails, admit it frankly and try another. But above all, try something."[12] And former President John F. Kennedy stated, "There are risks and costs to a program of action, but they are far less than long-range risks and costs of comfortable inaction."[13]

Further, we should recognize that failure is valuable because it is nature's way of guiding us down the right path. We would do well to follow the advice of John Dewey, who said, "Failure is instructive. The person who really thinks, learns quite as much from his failures as from his successes."[14] In the end, failure teaches us to recognize that experience is truly the best teacher.

Key Points

1. **Why is facing your fears helpful?**

   You cannot transcend what you do not confront. Fears can imprison you in your comfort zone and the WSC syndrome, causing you to be too afraid to risk making your life better. Additionally, you cannot learn anything if you do not accept the risks that come with trying to move forward.

2. **Why is facing your fears important to your family?**

   Your family, particularly your children, may unconsciously emulate your self-destructive fears. If you want your children to succeed, you must overcome your own fears.

3. How can you overcome fears?

By facing them, accepting responsibility for yourself, setting goals, and dedicating your efforts to achieving them.

4. When attempting to free yourself from the WSC syndrome, why is it important to slowly transition to risk taking?

Abandoning a comfort zone too quickly may trigger fear and paralysis. Transitioning to risk taking slowly allows you to adjust to the shift more easily.

5. Why is it important not to fear failure?

Fearing failure may discourage you from trying, thereby assuring defeat. Confronting adversity, on the other hand, helps develop the character needed to succeed.

6. Why is learning how to fail the first step in learning how to succeed?

When you understand how failure can teach you important lessons, you can more easily refuse to let it undermine your efforts to improve your life.

PART II

Taking Action

Chapter 11

FROM THOUGHTS TO EMPOWERMENT

A nod,
a bow,
and a tip of the lid
to the person
who coulda
and shoulda
and did.

—ROBERT BRAULT

Part 2 of this book examines the action and understanding required to successfully introduce the empowerment mindset into our daily lives. Chapter 11 provides an overview of how thoughts, influenced by attitudes and values, initiate a chain of causation leading ultimately to our destinies. Figure 11.1 illustrates the links in this chain.

An understanding of this progression helps to embed the empowerment mindset into our psyches. Once embedded, it can release the brakes that may be holding us back from acting on thoughts to realize success.

THE ROLE OF VALUES AND ATTITUDES IN DETERMINING THOUGHTS

Weakness in attitude becomes weakness in character.

—ALBERT EINSTEIN

Our thoughts are determined by our values and attitudes, which, in turn, impact how we think and act, so understanding how values and attitudes are obtained is critical. Values are fundamental, deeply held beliefs

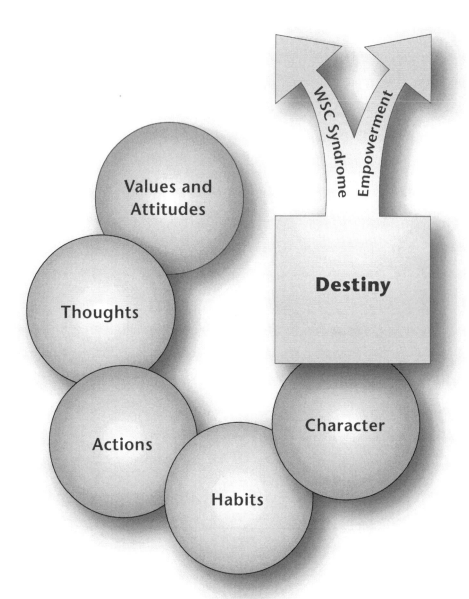

Figure 11.1 CHAIN OF CAUSATION LEADING TO DESTINY

that guide us through life, providing a moral compass that allows us to choose between right and wrong. Values are acquired from our parents, friends, teachers, religious leaders, and other people, as well as from environmental and cultural sources.

Attitudes are established ways of responding to people and situations based on the values we hold. They can emerge from genetic predispositions or personal observations, or they can be acquired from parents, teachers, or peers. Understanding that *we can change our lives by changing our attitudes, which alters our thoughts,* is fundamental to the empowerment mindset.

Some specific foundational values and attitudes that can help us use the empowerment mindset to improve our lives are:

◆ **Gratitude.** Gratitude is one of the most powerful foundational attitudes that can help us achieve success and happiness. Being grateful means being thankful for the blessings we receive in life. Acknowledging our blessings helps us reduce stress, maintain good health, enjoy life more fully, and retain a positive attitude so we not only send positive energy to others but receive positive energy for ourselves as well.

◆ **Humility.** Humility is another powerful foundational attitude that can help us succeed. When we are humble, we do not think less of ourselves but think of ourselves less. People who practice humility are able to more readily empathize with others and have compassion for themselves and others. Humility allows us to maintain a realistic estimate of our importance so we avoid becoming so self-absorbed that we fail to appreciate life's gifts. This, in turn, helps us maintain the positive attitude necessary to move forward and create more meaningful and productive lives.

◆ **Trust.** Trust is a foundational attitude that can help us improve our chances of success and happiness by allowing us to establish meaningful relationships. We should at least be able to have a healthy level of trust among our family, friends, and close associates, and should seek out people who share this disposition.

◆ **Integrity and honesty.** Integrity and honesty are two foundational values that help ensure trust and thus contribute to our potential for creating successful relationships and situations. They also assist us in overcoming denial about any obstructions so we will face our problems and begin to move forward.

	AGE
Failed in business	22
Ran for Illinois State Legislature—defeated	23
Again failed in business	24
Elected to Illinois State Legislature	25
Sweetheart Ann Rutledge died of typhoid fever	26
Suffered a nervous breakdown	27
Defeated for speaker	29
Defeated for elector	31
Defeated for Congress	34
Elected to Congress	37
Defeated for Congress	39
Defeated for Senate	46
Defeated for vice president	47
Defeated for Senate	49
Elected sixteenth president of the United States	51

Figure 11.2 ABRAHAM LINCOLN'S FAILURES AND SUCCESSES

◆ **Kindness.** Kindness is a foundational value that can serve as a bridge connecting us with other people. When we show kindness to people, others are kind to us, giving us positive energy to support our own development and successes.

◆ **Strength of mind.** Strength of mind is a foundational attitude that can help us face fear and adversity. By persistently pursuing our goals, we reinforce our strength of mind so we can continue to move forward on our quest for happiness and success.

◆ **Perseverance.** Perseverance is a foundational value that can keep us from succumbing to discouragement as we continue to pursue our goals despite temporary failures. The importance of this value can easily be seen by examining the lives of people who became famous or successful only after considerable perseverance. A good example is the life of the sixteenth president of the United States, Abraham Lincoln, whose failures and successes at various stages are listed in figure 11.2 on page 108. To keep moving forward, we must focus on actions most important to achieving the goals we have set, pursuing them with the attitude of utmost perseverance.

The Role and Impact of Thoughts

I have always thought the actions of men
the best interpreters of their thoughts.

—JOHN LOCKE

Thus far we have learned that thoughts can impact us in the following ways:

◆ Cause us to become what we think about most of the time, which is why toxic thoughts can sicken us physically and spiritually, potentially leading to emotional sabotage that worsens our situation

◆ Cause us to be self-absorbed and self-centered:

   ◆ Blocking awareness of our surroundings and blinding us to the interests and needs of others

   ◆ Posing an obstacle to communicating and empathizing with others

   ◆ Resulting in risk-averse behavior when action is needed

◆ Become habitual, making it necessary for us to go beyond our comfort zone and acquire a mind of reinvention to reach our potential

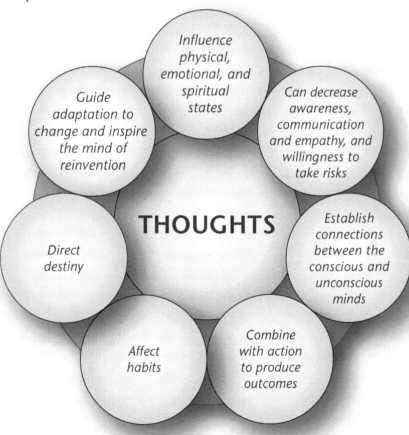

Figure 11.3 THE ROLE OF THOUGHTS

♦ Be instrumental in programming the subconscious mind to achieve goals

Because of the extraordinary power of thoughts, we need to be very mindful of what we think. Thoughts crystallize into words, then initiate actions. While some people's thought patterns are positive and produce constructive results in their daily lives, many individuals, especially those trapped in the WSC syndrome, harbor negative thought patterns that prohibit them from reaching their goals. Such individuals need to learn how to switch from negative to positive thinking.

THOUGHTS AND THE LAW OF ATTRACTION

Ask and it will be given to you;
seek and you will find;
knock and the door will be opened to you.
For everyone who asks receives; the one who seeks finds;
and to the one who knocks, the door will be opened.

—MATTHEW 7:7–8

The law of attraction asserts that positive thinking and visualization attract positive outcomes, while negative thinking and visualization attract negative results. Thinking is like beaming radio waves out into the cosmos at various frequencies revealed to us by our emotions. Feelings of pessimism and unhappiness mean we are emitting a frequency that draws negative things to us, while feelings of optimism and happiness mean we are emitting a frequency that attracts positive things to us.

The emotion of love is the most powerful positive frequency a human can emit, while hate is thought to be the most powerful negative frequency. This explains why dwelling on negative thoughts can lead to poor outcomes and why thinking positive thoughts can improve our lives. To make constructive changes in our lives, we need to alter our frequency by modifying our thoughts.

THOUGHTS AND ACTION

Our lives are not determined by what happens to us,
but by how we react to what happens;
not by what life brings us but by the attitude we bring to life.
A positive attitude causes a chain reaction of
positive thoughts, events, and outcomes.
It is a catalyst, a spark that creates extraordinary results.

—ANONYMOUS

We can use the law of attraction to assist us in turning positive thoughts into actions that lead to achieving our goals. To activate the law of attraction, after specifying a goal we wish to attain we need to: visualize it with the clearest possible mental image; commit to it and reinforce our commitment to achieving the goal; emotionalize the outcome by envisioning the positive feelings we will have upon attaining the goal; believe in our ability to reach the goal; and then actualize the goal by thinking and behaving as if it were accomplished while consciously programming our subconscious minds to take action.

Many people familiar with the popular literature about the law of attraction have the misconception that all they have to do to improve their lives is think positive thoughts. However, it is misleading to assume that merely thinking positively about an outcome will lead to successful results. In contrast, the empowerment mindset directs us to follow up all positive thinking and visualization with a carefully planned course of action.

It is common to hear businessmen who suspect empty posturing say, "Bullshit talks and money walks." This implies that accomplishment requires action and some risk, rather than just talk. Those who do not achieve their desired results usually have a list of excuses for doing nothing, while high achievers focus immediately on taking action on worthwhile ideas. We cannot reinvent our lives if we expect someone else to do it for us or if we live in the past.

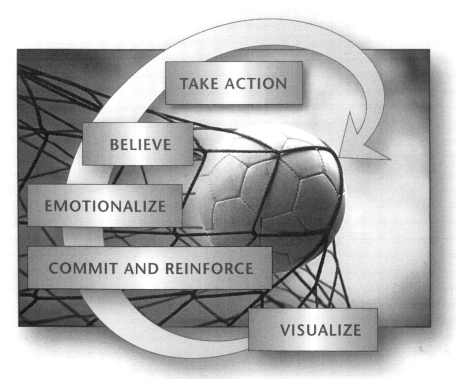

Figure 11.4 ACTIVATING THE LAW OF ATTRACTION TO ACHIEVE A GOAL

Consequently, in adopting an empowerment mindset we need to not only visualize the goals we want to attain but take the necessary action to reach them. In fact, we must continuously remind ourselves of the importance of this "action orientation," remaining focused on the action that should follow any commitment to a goal. Acting on our ideas and intentions, rather than making excuses or waiting for others to help us, underscores our resolve, forces us to accept responsibility for our behavior, and helps us achieve our goals. We can maintain our empowerment mindset and reach goals even faster if we are proactive—that is, looking forward to the future, focusing on what can be changed, accepting responsibility for our behavior, and taking charge to improve our circumstances before facing potentially new problems.

Figure 11.5 BEING PROACTIVE

HABITS OF THOUGHT OR BEHAVIOR

We are what we repeatedly do.
Excellence, then, is not an act, but a habit.

—ARISTOTLE

Understanding how habits of thought or behavior can undermine our efforts represents another critical aspect of reaching our empowerment potential. Habits are acquired patterns of thought or behavior that, as a result of being repeated regularly, become involuntary, such as looking in the rearview mirror while driving before we change lanes. Some common bad habits of thought that can undermine our empowerment were discussed in chapter 2. It has also been shown how such negative habits of thought must be replaced with more positive ones, as well as positive associations with people and environments to ensure our optimal empowerment potential.

Some common bad habits of behavior that many would recognize are overeating, gambling, smoking, drinking alcohol excessively, using drugs, gossiping, lying, cheating, squandering time, and spending money unnecessarily. Some good habits of behavior are exercising regularly and practicing moderation in eating, drinking, and spending.

As bad habits of thought or behavior become hardwired into our psychological makeup, they become difficult to break without considerable effort. Ultimately "where there is a will, there is a way" to alter habits—we just need to muster the courage and commitment to making the desired changes.

COUNTERING BAD HABITS WITH GOOD ONES

Thoughts and Character
Mind is the Master-power that molds and makes,
And Man is Mind, and ever more he takes
The Tool of Thought, and shaping what he wills,
brings forth a thousand joys, a thousand ills.
He thinks in secret and it comes to pass;
Environment is but his looking-glass.

—JAMES ALLEN

People often believe that their character has been conclusively shaped by various genetic, environmental, and experiential factors and that they must live with their fate. However, the character we have is made up of our habits, which can be altered. Habits are in our subconscious minds and surface to express our characters when the appropriate cues occur. Thus by changing our habits we can change our characters and, subsequently, our destinies.

Key Points

1. Why are values and attitudes important?
   They determine thoughts and are thus critical to achieving goals.

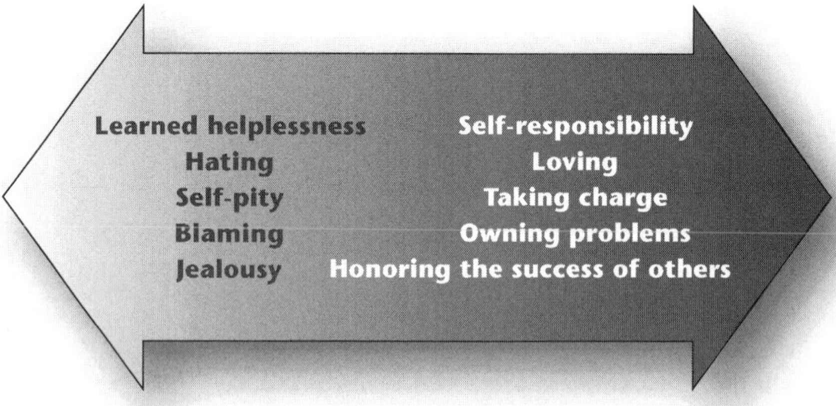

Figure 11.6 COUNTERING BAD HABITS WITH GOOD ONES

Within the figure:

Learned helplessness	Self-responsibility
Hating	Loving
Self-pity	Taking charge
Blaming	Owning problems
Jealousy	Honoring the success of others

2. What are some benefits of the foundational attitude of gratitude?

The ability to appreciate your blessings in life helps you reduce stress, maintain good health, enjoy life more fully, and maintain the positive attitude necessary to receive positive energy in return, facilitating beneficial change.

3. Why is humility a useful value to cultivate?

Humility helps you empathize with other people and have compassion for yourself and others so you avoid focusing excessively on yourself and thus develop more meaningful relationships.

4. What is the significance of trust, integrity, and honesty?

They are important for establishing successful relationships with others so they will be inclined to support you.

5. Why is cultivating kindness helpful?

When you show kindness to others, they are kind to you, giving you positive energy to support your success.

6. Why persevere in the face of adversity even when you don't think you can make a difference?

Through perseverance you gradually increase your strength of mind and thus your ability to succeed.

7. What is the first and most critical link in the chain of causation that determines your destiny?

Your thoughts.

8. How do positive thoughts influence a person's well-being?

They are the key to achieving positive results.

9. Why are negative thought patterns harmful?

They may prevent you from achieving the success you desire.

10. How can you switch to positive thinking?

By replacing negative thoughts with positive thoughts, expecting the best, refusing to accept defeat, believing in your power to solve your problems, and developing a peaceful mind.

11. What is the law of attraction?

It asserts that positive thinking and visualizing positive results attracts positive outcomes, while negative thinking and visualizing negative results attracts negative outcomes.

12. How can you activate the law of attraction to act positively and achieve your goals?

By asking for and visualizing outcomes and by believing you have already achieved them.

13. Why is it so important to take action to achieve goals after committing to them?

Taking action on ideas and intentions underscores your resolve, forces you to accept responsibility for your behavior, and helps you achieve your goals sooner than if you made excuses or waited for others to help you.

14. **How can you make the law of attraction a habit?**

By reviewing a day's events and visualizing the way you wanted them to go; developing a positive self-image; treating yourself with love and respect; focusing on what you appreciate about those closest to you; believing in what you are seeking to accomplish; and dwelling on health rather than sickness.

15. **What does it mean to be proactive?**

To look to the future, focus on what you can change, accept responsibility for your behavior, and take charge to improve your circumstances rather than waiting for others to do so.

16. **What are habits and why are they important?**

They are either beneficial or harmful patterns of thought or behavior acquired as a result of being repeated regularly and thus having become involuntary.

17. **How can you change bad habits?**

Replace them with good habits and reward your successes.

Law of Empowerment 7

Changing our lives means changing our thoughts. Our thoughts are the most critical link in the chain of factors that determine our destinies.

Law of Empowerment 8

Empowering ourselves to achieve greater success means harnessing the power of values and attitudes that support our endeavors and help us achieve our goals.

Chapter 12

EMPOWERMENT FUNDAMENTALS

Never be afraid to try something new.
Remember, amateurs built the ark.
Professionals built the Titanic.

— UNKNOWN

To turbocharge our success, we need to have a comprehensive understanding of the fundamental ideas that form the bedrock of the empowerment mindset: knowing our life's purpose, understanding the power of health, making sustained efforts, and acquiring skills and strategies.

KNOWING OUR LIFE'S PURPOSE

Don't ask yourself what the world needs.
Ask yourself what makes you come alive, and then go and do it.
Because what the world needs is people who have come alive.

—HAROLD THURMAN WHITMAN

To use our empowerment mindset to attain success and well-being, we need to know our life's purpose so we can apply our empowerment skills to realize it. We can tell whether what we are doing is attuned with our life's purpose if it makes us feel we are "in the zone" and brings us happiness. A while ago I found that my life's purpose was to help people assist themselves by giving them the knowledge to do so. Therefore, when I am able to write to further my life's purpose my mind is focused so that time flies by, I seem to have an unending reserve of momentum to achieve my goals, and I am happy. When we are aligned with our life's purpose, we do not waste time or effort in attracting the opportunities and resources to follow it. Since finding our life's purpose is one of the most critical things we can do in life, it will be addressed more fully in chapter 15.

UNDERSTANDING THE POWER OF HEALTH

To keep the body in good health is a duty, for otherwise we shall not be able to trim the lamp of wisdom and keep our mind strong and clear. Water surrounds the lotus flower but does not wet its petals.

—BUDDHA

Physical well-being is important for our empowerment potential since it is the foundation for mental, emotional, and spiritual health. Because good health is one of the greatest assets people possess—some even say the "body is a temple"—it is important to treat our bodies with care and respect.

Statistics showing that the preventable health problems of obesity, diabetes, and cardiovascular disease have reached epidemic proportions, provide plenty of evidence that health is one of the most common matters people take for granted. There are many ways people routinely abuse their bodies, including getting insufficient exercise and sleep, overeating, becoming emotionally stressed, and overmedicating, all of which can undermine the energy and strength needed to succeed. People also rely too heavily on advances in medical science, technology, and prescription drugs to compensate for not taking preventative healthcare measures.

For inspiration on the many ways to appreciate physical health, it is helpful to consider those whose health has been compromised in some manner, such as due to a disabling disease, the inability to see or hear, or chronic pain. Because poor health can severely limit our options to achieve goals and improve our lives, we should make every effort to cherish and maintain our well-being by adopting healthy lifestyle habits, such as restricting our intake of calories, eating nutritious foods, and incorporating regular exercise into daily routines.

MAKING SUSTAINED EFFORTS

In all human affairs there are efforts and there are results,
and the strength of the effort is the measure of the result.

—JAMES ALLEN

To adopt an empowerment mindset and realize our goals beyond the WSC syndrome, we must make sustained efforts, while managing expectations so we remain flexible enough to adapt to a range of possible results. Hard work is an inescapable requirement needed to attain any accomplishment. And the rewards we receive are always directly related to the efforts we make.

In contrast to the current tendency in our culture to downplay the virtue and necessity of hard work to succeed, earlier generations well understood the value of it. Hard work means focusing on the task at hand, getting it done as quickly as possible, and sacrificing time we might have spent doing something more immediately enjoyable for a worthy long-term goal. It allows us to be self-reliant, self-responsible, escape the economic dependency trap, validate our self-worth, and satisfy the wish we have to be valued and appreciated by our families, friends, and communities.

In considering how we want to expend our efforts, we should realize that our rewards come not only in the form of money or material possessions but also in the satisfaction achieved in accomplishing something (even if we fail) or in increasing our knowledge, self-confidence, and sense of self-worth. For example, I will always remember how good it made me feel as a boy to be told by my mom that I had done a good job with household chores, or the satisfaction I experienced when after six months of digging a basement under our house my dad rewarded me with a little red bicycle.

Even though hard work is usually rewarded not only financially but socially and psychologically, managing our expectations of specific results helps us mentally prepare for a variety of potential outcomes and sustain our empowerment mindset for future efforts. Despite the fact that people automatically build expectations around desired outcomes, we can manage our expectations by either trying to remain unattached to them or cultivating a flexible attitude toward them by thinking through a variety of potential outcomes in advance so we are prepared to adapt to a range of possible results.

ACQUIRING SKILLS AND STRATEGIES

You are the embodiment of the information you choose to accept and act upon.
To change your circumstances
you need to change your thinking and subsequent actions.

—ADLIN SINCLAIR

Successful people possess skills and strategies anyone can adopt, but to do so requires an eagerness to learn, hard work, dedication, and a willingness to gain knowledge from early failures. With such skills and strategies, people are like the proverbial falling cat that always lands on its feet. One of the most fundamental skills learned by all successful people is to take total responsibility for their lives, which includes: not complaining, giving excuses, and blaming; adapting responses to get different outcomes; and adopting better habits.

Some other key empowerment skills are the following:

◆ **Ability to prioritize.** We cannot do everything, so to achieve success we must prioritize what we wish to accomplish, focusing first on activities most critical to achieving our major goals, then on activities related to our minor goals. When we prioritize our goals, we commit our energies to those activities most significant for success.

◆ **Ability to focus.** Another valuable skill that can increase our chances for success is the ability to focus our energy on the goal we are trying to reach while filtering out any distractions, resulting in efficient use of our time and resources. Learning to focus at an early age saves individuals an enormous amount of time and effort later, when facing new challenges. However, it is also entirely possible to learn to focus later in life, although it may take more practice.

◆ **Self-discipline.** Disciplining ourselves is yet another useful skill for successfully pursuing our goals. It means being determined to perform any tasks necessary to reach our objectives and then doing them. Self-discipline can be learned at home, in school, or through any endeavor that fosters the ability to perform repetitive activities aimed at achieving long-term goals. Part of the value of developing self-discipline is that once it is learned in one area of our lives it can be transferred to other areas.

◆ **Ability to communicate.** The ability to communicate is another essential skill for success because it is through relationships with others that we are able to achieve our goals. To develop relationships that foster success, it is important to realize that communication is a two-way process and thus listen respectfully and empathize with others' positions, paying attention to both feeling and meaning in order to comprehend the emotional content being conveyed. When we do this, we are in a much better position to communicate with others in a way that leads to mutual respect and cooperation, increasing our potential for reaching our goals.

◆ **A win/win perspective.** Many people cannot achieve success because instead of having a win/win perspective, thinking in a way that expands their options, they have a win/lose perspective, thinking competitively in a way that limits their options. When we have a win/lose perspective, we think there is a finite number of benefits and the winner gets them all, rather than envisioning an infinite number of benefits in which all can share. When we approach situations believing that no one has to lose—essentially imagining the "pie" as big enough for everyone to have a slice— we build relationships based on mutual respect that are far more fulfilling and enduring than those based on a competitive perspective. When we use win/win thinking, we optimize our chances for beneficial outcomes and develop character traits that will best serve us in achieving goals and securing success and happiness.

◆ **Ability to network.** Individuals all have different talents and skill sets, so it makes sense that when people pool their knowledge, experience, and networks to work cooperatively, they create synergies, or mutually advantageous connections, that enhance their efficiency and potential for success. Consequently, our ability to network can be an important skill for empowerment and achievement of goals.

◆ **Financial literacy and money management.** Financial literacy and money management are significant empowerment skills because to escape habitual failure and the WSC syndrome it is important to learn how to deal effectively with money and understand its proper role in life.

Many people associate success with the acquisition of money and material possessions, having been conditioned to believe that the "good life" consists of making as much money as possible and ostentatiously displaying it. Our Western culture gets caught up in keeping up with the Joneses—behavior that has led to the largest per capita debt in the history of civilization and is putting enormous strain on poor and middle-class families. In a society where 70 percent of our GDP is derived from personal consumption, corporate and government messaging is aimed at reinforcing consumptive behavior. While financial resources clearly affect our lives in significant ways, having money is not the only requirement for achieving success and happiness. Rather, we should appreciate the value of money, given our situations, while balancing financial concerns with other important needs and interests.

Money is clearly necessary for survival if we are poor. Money is very important for providing for basic needs, or as a way out of economic dependency. Beyond this, we require money to increase our options for material well-being and comfort, neither of which, however, automatically leads to greater happiness.

Higher income earners should view money as merely a tool and not an end in itself. Making money solely for the sake of having more revenue is a spiritually empty pursuit. While money can provide greater opportunities, it cannot supply happiness, fill our hearts with love, nourish our spirits, or impart wisdom. These essentials come from within and from perceiving our connection to the broader context of nature and spirit—from meaningful social relations, a sense of community, freedom from fear, and having a life purpose.

Moreover, making money dishonestly can rob us of our peace of mind and the satisfaction derived from authentic achievement. Then, too, having money but using it in an undisciplined manner can wreak havoc on our personal and family lives.

If becoming self-responsible and escaping the WSC syndrome are important to us, managing our financial resources should be at the forefront of our skill set. Depleting cash reserves, borrowing imprudently, deferring critical investments, and relying excessively on external resources is a recipe for a serious day of financial reckoning, for individuals as well as for nations. A good guideline to follow when it comes to managing money is: If you don't have the money, don't spend it. Today, when credit cards make it easy to borrow money constantly and stores finance purchases for 0 percent interest, we have to be mindful of the dictum that guided our parents and grandparents in their financial decisions: If you don't spend it, you don't have to earn it. Unfortunately, many people ignore this dictum and are forced to face the unwavering maxim of modern economics: You have to pay back borrowed money, which involves earning more than is needed for current expenditures. If leading a less stressful life is important, then it is unwise to buy things that will needlessly add to our financial burdens.

To manage our finances, it is helpful to learn to create a budget and live within it. A budget—an itemized summary of intended expenditures for a given period of time—provides us with the information necessary to determine our financial status so we can avoid excessive debt and remain freer in life. To make a budget, simply record income minus expenses as shown in figure 12.1.

Learning all these empowerment fundamentals enables us to move forward on our path to develop an empowerment mindset and achieve success in our endeavors.

Key Points

1. Why is it important to determine your life's purpose?

   It is critical to providing direction for everything you do and gives you focus so you do not waste precious time and resources.

2. What are some prevalent but preventable health problems in modern society?

   Obesity, diabetes, and cardiovascular disease.

3. Why is it important to cherish your physical health?

   Physical health is the foundation for mental, emotional, and spiritual health, and critical for maintaining an empowerment mindset to achieve success and happiness.

4. What is the relationship between hard work and rewards?

   Hard work increases the likelihood of achieving rewards and can be its own reward.

5. Why is it important to manage expectations when undertaking a course of action?

   Thinking through a variety of potential outcomes in advance will prepare you to adapt to a range of possible results.

6. What are some fundamental skills and strategies needed to achieve an empowerment mindset and become successful?

   The ability to prioritize, the ability to focus, self-discipline, the

MONTH	1	2	3	4	5	6	7	8	9	10	11	12
INCOME												
Salary												
Family allowance												
Other												
TOTAL MONTHLY INCOME												
EXPENSES												
Mortgage/rent												
Electricity												
Gas												
Telephone												
Cable												
Home insurance												
Water/sewer												
Property tax												
Groceries												
House maintenance												
Newspapers												
Magazines												
Health insurance												
Dental expenses												
Music lessons												
Lessons for children												
Clothing												
Vehicle insurance												
Vehicle expenses												
Personal insurance												
Personal loans												
Entertainment												
Family gifts												
Holiday costs												
Miscellaneous												
TOTAL MONTHLY EXPENSES												
BALANCE (monthly leftover)												

Figure 12.1 SAMPLE BUDGET SHEET

ability to communicate, a win/win perspective, the ability to network, financial literacy, and money management.

7. Why is it helpful to prioritize your activities?

When you prioritize your activities, you commit your energies to tasks that are most significant for success.

8. Why is learning to focus a useful skill?

Focusing on goals you are trying to achieve results in efficient use of your time and resources.

9. How does self-discipline contribute to success?

It helps you focus more effectively on achieving your goals.

10. Why is listening a big part of communicating?

It allows you to comprehend the emotional content conveyed by others, leading to mutual respect and cooperation, and increasing your potential for reaching your goals.

11. Why is a win/win perspective important?

It encourages you to think there are an infinite number of benefits for everyone to share, rather than thinking competitively and assuming there are a finite number of benefits and the winner gets them all.

12. What are synergies and how do they influence us?

They are mutually advantageous connections created when people work cooperatively that enhance their efficiency and potential for success.

13. Should acquiring money be a major focus of your life?

Yes and no. Money is important for providing basic needs and to increase your options for material well-being and comfort, but becoming wealthier cannot provide happiness, nourish your spirit, or impart wisdom.

14. What is most important for happiness?

Meaningful social relations, a sense of community, freedom from fear, and having a life purpose.

15. Why is a budget valuable?

It allows you to determine your financial status and plan your finances so you can avoid excessive debt and remain freer in life.

Law of Empowerment 9

Hard work and sustained efforts are necessary to achieve success. In everything we do, the rewards we receive are equal to the efforts we invest.

Chapter 13

OVERCOMING
PSYCHOLOGICAL BARRIERS

*Obstacles are those things a person sees
when he takes his eyes off his goal.*

—E. JOSEPH COSMAN

Adopting the empowerment mindset requires us to deal with issues of denial, face the reality of our situation, and "own" our problems by accepting responsibility for our lives, a process illustrated in figure 13.1.

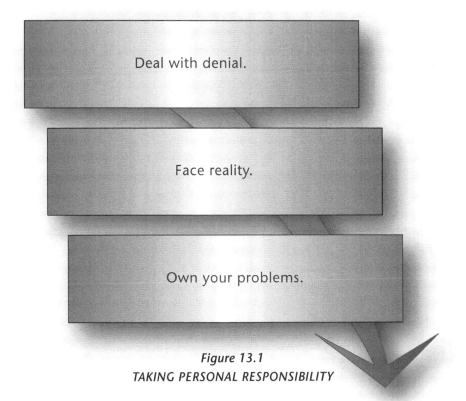

Deal with denial.

Face reality.

Own your problems.

Figure 13.1
TAKING PERSONAL RESPONSIBILITY

DEALING WITH DENIAL

To regret one's own experiences is to arrest one's own development.
To deny one's own experiences is to put a lie into the lips of one's life.
It is no less than a denial of the soul.

—OSCAR WILDE

People trapped in the WSC syndrome are often in denial about their situation. Denial occurs when our minds keep us blind to the things we don't want to see because we are unable to handle them. Denial has been defined as "an unconscious and natural coping mechanism that allows us to refuse to identify or acknowledge the existence or significance of unpleasant external circumstances or internal feelings and thoughts."[1]

According to Ken Seeley, author and former meth addict who founded Intervention-911, we are all in denial about something that is holding us back from living life to the fullest, such as some type of abuse, disorder, addiction, health issue, or truth about ourselves and those around us.[2] There are many reasons for denial, such as wanting to avoid problems or the work involved in solving them, needing to feel in control, or wishing to avoid blame for mistakes. For those stuck in the WSC syndrome, it may simply be too unpleasant to face the fact that their behaviors or attitudes lead to habitual failure. However, remaining in denial about any challenging circumstance or behavior makes it impossible to create a more successful and fulfilling life. Consequently, we must first identify any situation, attitude, or behavior that is keeping us stuck in denial before we can take the next step of fully facing the reality of our circumstances.

FACING REALITY

Life is not a problem to be solved, but a reality to be experienced.

—SØREN KIERKEGAARD

It may be very difficult for individuals trapped in the WSC syndrome to face the reality that their attitudes and behaviors may be causing or contributing to their negative circumstances or to admit that a particular situation is creating feelings of inadequacy and powerlessness. But while some people experiencing failure may find emotional relief in denial or in escapist behavior such as substance abuse it is more productive for them to face the reality of their circumstances so they can chart a course to move forward.

Facing reality does not mean accepting responsibility for a particular problem (especially if we did not cause it) or forgiving the responsible people or circumstances. The goal of facing reality is to simply accept that it exists, realizing that shutting our minds to it makes no difference to its impact, regardless of its cause. Once we are able to accept unalterable facts and let go of resentment and focus on the past, we free ourselves to look to the future and prepare to improve our lives.

OWNING PROBLEMS

It is not because things are difficult that we do not dare;
it is because we do not dare that things are difficult.

—SENECA

The view that someone else or some external situation has trapped us or is the cause of our difficulties is a common, albeit unproductive, standpoint. But such blaming cannot fix problems and instead leads to a perpetual state of grievance that can become an all too convenient explanation for everything unpleasant or challenging that happens to us, keeping us from taking responsibility for our own lives.

The truth is that even when problems may have been caused by others we have to accept responsibility for our current situation and focus on thoughts and activities geared toward moving us forward. Only we can genuinely have our self-interest in mind; and, ultimately, only we can solve our problems by acknowledging the harm they cause us, realizing that only we can deal with them, and making a commitment to move forward. Once we have embraced this approach of owning our problems, the futility of blaming others for our circumstances or expecting others to solve our problems becomes apparent.

Dealing with denial, facing reality, and owning our problems leads to automatically assuming self-responsibility for our happiness rather than blaming our unhappiness on external events that we cannot control. The result is a more successful and happier life, and one more in alignment with an empowerment mindset.

Key Points

1. What are some ways to overcome psychological barriers to adopting an empowerment mindset?

   Dealing with denial, facing reality, and owning problems by accepting responsibility for your life.

2. What does facing the reality of your situation mean?

   Experiencing the reality of it without denial.

3. Why should you own your problems?

   Because it frees you from denial and allows you to take responsibility for solving them, regardless of their source.

PART III

Developing a Strategic Plan

Key to Empowerment

FINDING THE POWER

In the darkness, I sought the glow—
A blind one's plea, the path to show:

Grandfathers,
I seek your light,
Heavy burden
Cosmic plight.

Summer sunset,
Winter moon,
Bathe the spirit
Warm cocoon.

Ancient ancestors,
I beseech,
Power eludes
Out of reach.

The answer came, to my surprise—
A way forward, to hidden eyes:

Little one,
What you seek,
Call to heart
Not for meek.

Babbling brook,

Curling wave,

Courage at hand

Yourself to save.

Humble being,

Make no mistake,

Light of rapture

Yours to take.

Gentle breeze,

Autumn wind,

Unfurl the sail

Do not rescind.

Lost soul,

The key's within,

Unlock your fate

A life to win.

Now I know, Nature's ghost

Will exorcise, to be the most.

Chapter 14

UNDERSTANDING
STRATEGIC PLANNING

He who fails to plan, plans to fail.

—PROVERB

In Part 3, the rubber of ideas meets the road of reality. Through putting together the pieces of the puzzle of empowerment, we are standing up and declaring that we count for something—our sense of self-worth and our future well-being depend on our unwavering courage at this point. Like early Spanish conquistador Hernán Cortés, who destroyed his ships upon landing in Veracruz, Mexico, so that there was no option of going back until he succeeded with his mission, we must act decisively to burn the "ships" of our bad habits of thought and behavior that may tempt us to return to our comfort zones and can never lead to our empowerment and success.

It is time to call on the spirit warrior within us to unsheath the sword of our potential and begin cutting through the obstacles blocking our success. We all have the same power, but more rewards come to those who boldly step out of their comfort zone, assert their power, and say yes to change and a better future.

To control our destiny, we first need to discover our life's purpose then make a strategic plan, which includes determining our strategic vision and establishing our goals, and finally execute our plan to achieve those goals and fulfill our life's purpose. As motivational speaker Jim Rohn poignantly commented, "If you don't design your own life plan, chances are you'll fall into someone else's. And guess what they might have planned for you? Not much."[1]

In the business world, strategic planning is a management tool used to

Figure 14.1
PUTTING TOGETHER THE PIECES OF THE PUZZLE OF EMPOWERMENT

produce decisions and actions that guide how an organization defines itself, what it does, and its direction for the future. To determine its direction, the organization needs to assess where it stands, then ascertain where it wants to go and how it will get there. The resulting document is called a "strategic plan." The strategic plan concept is a powerful tool that can also be used to achieve personal goals.

To make our strategic plan, we must first discover our life's purpose in conjunction with objectively assessing and accepting our current circumstances; next, we must develop our strategic vision, based on circumstances we hope to manifest; and then we must establish the goals necessary to realize our strategic vision. Finally, we need to execute our strategic plan to reach our goals. As well, it is important to be aware that reality is continuously changing and that our strategic plan may have to be periodically adapted to remain relevant.

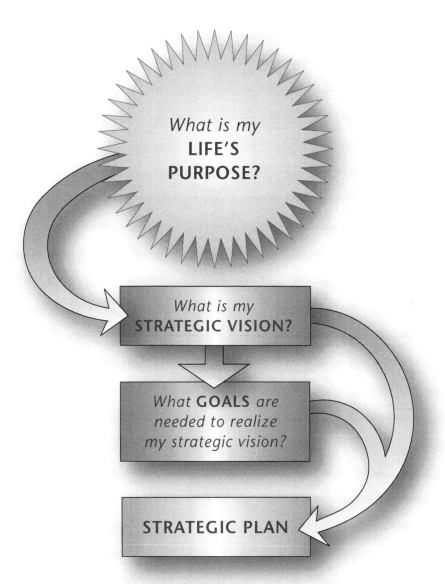

Figure 14.2 DEVELOPING A STRATEGIC PLAN

To dissipate doubt while determining our strategic vision, we must know specifically what we want and why we want it in the context of our life's purpose, and then describe the desirable circumstances as if they are certain to be attained. For example, a strategic vision for someone trapped in the WSC syndrome might be stated as: "I will be financially independent, earning over $100,000 within five years; able to provide my family with the material benefits, education, and quality of life needed to lead fulfilling and happy lives within two years; and have the self-responsibility and confidence to pursue a goal of helping others in the world through working in nonprofit organizations in three years."

In developing our strategic plan, we should expect to take sufficient time to carefully think through its elements to make sure it aligns with our life's purpose and capabilities. With a strategic plan, our time, hard work, and resources will be more effectively deployed. As well, the satisfaction of knowing we are the authors of our own success is a substantial reward in itself.

The chapters that follow provide specific details about discovering our life's purpose, developing a strategic vision, establishing goals, and making a strategic plan—the pieces of the empowerment puzzle required to successfully implement the empowerment mindset.

Key Points

1. What is a strategic plan?

A planning tool used to achieve your goals in the context of your life's purpose, consisting of a list of goals and a detailed breakdown of all the steps necessary to attain them.

2. Why should you have a strategic plan?

Because it is necessary to achieve your goals and thus control your own destiny.

3. What is a strategic vision?

A vision of future desirable circumstances you hope to manifest by developing and following a strategic plan.

Law of Empowerment 10

To control our destiny, we discover our life's purpose and develop a strategic plan for making our wishes a reality. In so doing we become the authors of our own success.

Chapter 15

DISCOVERING
OUR LIFE'S PURPOSE

If a man knows not what harbor he seeks,
any wind is the right wind.

—SENECA

The first component of a personal strategic plan is discovering our life's purpose. The tendency of many people to wander through life without a specific purpose is reflected in a scene in Lewis Carroll's *Alice in Wonderland* in which Alice reaches a forked road and asks the Cheshire Cat where she ought to go from there. He responds by asking Alice where she wants to go, and she replies, "I don't much care where." The Cheshire Cat then answers, "If you do not care or know where you are going, any road will get you there"[1]—a notion that can lead to confusion, as illustrated in figure 15.1.

Like Alice, many people do not know where they want to go in their lives. However, to attain success and happiness they need to discover their life's purpose, which will become the basis for developing a strategic plan for their future.

Our life's purpose is the most fundamental thing in our lives, providing the context for our strategic vision and the reasons for our goals. It explains *why* we are doing what we choose to do, while our strategic vision represents *what* we are doing with our lives and our goals reflect *how* we are doing it.[2]

Because discovering our life's purpose is one of the most critical things we can do, it may require a concerted effort over time. In following the guidelines presented in this chapter, we should not be concerned about whether our initial attempts are completely in line with our feelings regarding our life's purpose. Over time, with deep and sustained thought, and

Figure 15.1 NOT KNOWING WHERE YOU WANT TO GO IN LIFE

following the guidance of the heart, we will refine our views of our life's purpose. The important thing is to start thinking about what it may be so we can become future oriented and begin taking charge of our lives.

To begin, consider an analogy of the relationship between our life's purpose, strategic vision, and goals. Bob Proctor suggests that our life's purpose is like sun, the unmoving and unchanging stable element around which all the planets revolve, whereas our strategic vision is like the planets that revolve around the sun (our purpose).[3] In keeping with this analogy, I would add that our goals, which are dependent on our strategic vision, are like moons revolving around the planets, as seen in figure 15.2.

Another thing to keep in mind when defining our life's purpose is to look at our potential from the perspective of a child who sees everything as possible—as though limitations have not yet been imposed. If we can overcome poor habits of mind and behavior that ordinarily limit our perspective, then we should not let such limiting factors restrict our vision of what is possible for our reinvented selves and even consider the seemingly unattainable.

Our life's purpose arises from what is most meaningful to us expressed through our abilities and the activities we like best that can help contribute to a better world. According to Dr. Wayne Dyer, "Each child comes into the world born with 'secret orders,'"[4] which, according to motivational speaker and author Jack Canfield, underline the purpose behind everything we do.[5] Canfield further suggests that identifying, acknowledging, and honoring this purpose is perhaps the most important action successful peo-

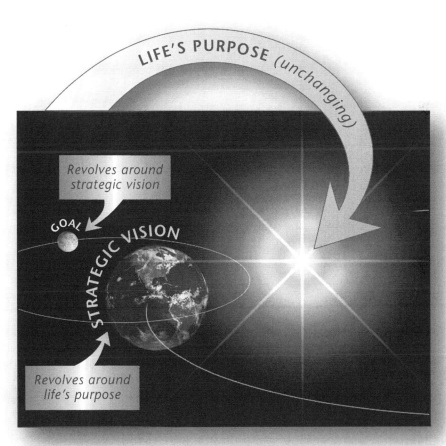

Figure 15.2 THE STABLE ELEMENT IN OUR LIVES

ple take.[6] To be "on purpose" means we are doing what we love to do, doing what we're good at, and accomplishing what's important to us—an alignment that not only attracts people, resources, and opportunities to us, according to the law of attraction, but results in our actions serving others.

We are all born with an inner guidance system that tells us when we are on or off purpose, determined by the amount of joy we are experiencing, as the things that bring us greatest joy are in alignment with our life's purpose. This inner guidance system is the heart. So getting in touch with our hearts and embracing the open heart attitude, as described in chapter 6, are critical to ultimately discovering our life's purpose.

To find our life's purpose, we need to first take time to deeply reflect on what is most meaningful to us, what we feel we were put on earth to do, what qualities and abilities we have, and what activities bring us joy and could contribute to a better world. Next, it would help to complete the following Life Purpose Exercise (on a blank sheet of paper), as suggested by Canfield:

1. List two of your unique personal qualities, such as *enthusiasm* and *creativity*.

2. List one or two ways in which you enjoy expressing those qualities when interacting with others, such as *support* and *inspire*.

3. Assume the world is perfect right now. What does the world look like? How is everyone interacting? What does it feel like? Write the answer as a statement, in the present tense, describing the ultimate condition, the perfect world as you see it and feel it. Remember, a perfect world is a fun place to be.

    EXAMPLE: *Everyone is freely expressing their own unique talents. Everyone is working in harmony. Everyone is expressing love.*

4. Combine answers one, two, and three into a single statement.

EXAMPLE: *My purpose is to use my creativity and enthusiasm to support and inspire others to freely express their talents in a harmonious and loving way.*[7]

An alternative method for determining our life's purpose is to:

1. Identify what is meaningful to you and how you would like to express it in your life.

2. Imagine you can contribute to creating a better world.

3. Recognize the true you, in all aspects of your being, and become more of who you were truly meant to be.[8]

In addition, once we have a general idea of what our life's purpose may be, it is helpful to write a draft of our conclusions within a self-imposed time line, such as two days, to express our commitment to defining it. We should not worry if our draft is incomplete or not entirely correct—what matters is to show that we have started to take responsibility for identifying our life's purpose. Then over time we can refine it, adjusting ideas as our visualization of it evolves while listening to what our hearts tells us we were put on this earth to do.

In these ways, for example, I have determined that my life's purpose is to empower people to help themselves through common sense and kindness, by providing the knowledge to do so through my writing. As a poor Native American from a remote reserve community, I had to struggle mightily just to get an education, and so such a life purpose initially seemed like an impossible dream. However, I dared to dream like a child, and with the help of some good people, the courage of my convictions, and an extraordinary amount of hard work, I overcame my poor habits of thought and am now fulfilling my life's purpose.

Once we have determined our life's purpose, we can figure out how to spend most of our time doing that activity for our job. We shouldn't allow ourselves to believe we can never follow this path because we are too busy making a living, looking after our family, or involved in other obligations.

Such negative thinking undermines positive expectations and can impede our progress in developing a strategic plan to pursue our life's purpose.

Key Points

1. **Why is it important to discover your life's purpose?**

   You are more likely to be successful and happy because your activities will be more focused and you will feel more fulfilled.

2. **How can you discover your life's purpose?**

   By determining what is most meaningful to you as expressed through your abilities and the activities you like best that can contribute to a better world.

3. **How can you tell when you are following the path of your life's purpose?**

   You will experience joy and a sense of fulfillment.

Chapter 16

DEVELOPING A STRATEGIC VISION

Strategic planning is worthless—
unless there is first a strategic vision.

—JOHN NAISBITT

The first component of a strategic plan is a strategic vision. Our strategic vision provides a picture of how to fulfill our life's purpose. It focuses on what and who we want to become at a set time in the future. While our strategic vision must be in line with our life's purpose, it is based on our personal values and beliefs and represents our highest priorities. Our strategic vision allows us to develop goals that act as yardsticks to measure our progress. It should be specific or we will be unable to develop goals to achieve it. Though it can help us envision the future, it must be grounded in the present. In essence, it is a statement of who we are and who we are becoming—the framework for creating our future success and happiness.

Our strategic vision may change over time as we accomplish the objectives set out initially or need to adapt it to new circumstances. In addition, we should not be misled into believing that our strategic vision is the end result when it is only the map for reaching individual goals. We still must take appropriate action to achieve our goals.

Finding our life's purpose leads to our strategic vision, and our strategic vision, in turn, leads to our goals. Our life's purpose is the "why" of our strategic planning process; our strategic vision is the "what"; and our goals are the "how," the concrete targets we use to achieve elements of our strategic vision. In effect, we express our life's purpose through our strategic vision and goals, as illustrated in figure 16.1.

To explain the difference between a strategic vision and goals, personal development teacher Bob Proctor describes a multicity trip by car across America. The act of arranging the itinerary—choosing the cities through which to travel—corresponds to creating the strategic vision, while the cities on the itinerary represent the goals.[1]

Another way to understand the distinction between a strategic vision and goals is to imagine a person whose life's purpose is: "I want to use my athletic abilities to be a world-class athlete in basketball and represent my country in the Olympics, become a professional player, and use my spare time to be a role model for children and youth" (the "why"). Their strategic vision might then be: "I will make the Olympic team in four years while using the interim period to finish my education and be selected by a college with a high-level basketball program in two years, and then I will make it onto a team in the NBA or other professional league within five years" (the "what"). And their goals might be to make it onto a college team, be selected for the Olympics, and then be hired for a professional team (the "how"). As figure 16.1 shows, our strategic vision is the key connector between our life's purpose and our daily goals.

Our strategic vision is very personal and should therefore be based on our own expectations, not those of others. We should not worry about what other people think of our strategic vision because it is related to what brings us the greatest joy, not someone else. As well, career/life coach Cecile Peterkin suggests that an effective strategic vision should reflect all the important elements of our lives and careers—how we want to be, what we want to do, how we want to feel, what we want to own, and with whom we want to associate.[2]

To help determine and realize our strategic vision, it is helpful to go through the process outlined in chapter 8 of programming our subconscious minds with our conscious minds by visualizing, committing

LIFE'S
PURPOSE

Why?

STRATEGIC VISION
Plan for fulfilling our life's purpose

What?

GOALS
Targets for implementing our strategic vision

How?

Figure 16.1
RELATIONSHIP AMONG KEY ELEMENTS OF EMPOWERMENT MINDSET

and reinforcing, emotionalizing, believing, and actualizing. The action required to implement our strategic vision comes when we identify our goals and create a detailed strategic plan that sets out the time line and success measurements required to achieve them. Using the example of the aspiring basketball star above, the results might be as depicted in figure 16.2.

To clarify our strategic vision and express conviction for pursuing goals to manifest it, it is also useful to write a strategic vision statement. Some examples of simple strategic vision statements are:

◆ In ten years, I want to be the president of my company.

◆ Within one year, I want to be physically fit and able to run five miles three times a week. I also want to do one fun activity per day. In two years, I want to have completed my degree.

◆ In five years, I want to win the Olympic gold medal for the 100-meter sprint. I want to look up at the crowd cheering in the stadium and feel a tremendous pride as I listen to my country's national anthem being played.[3]

A straightforward method for writing a vision statement is as follows:

◆ Write down five or six basic nonnegotiable values.

◆ Write down your passions, your dreams, your needs, and your strengths.

◆ Write your strategic vision statement in the first person using the preceding information. Be specific, set a time frame, and articulate the statement in such a way that it can be evaluated and measured.[4]

Developing our strategic vision is an essential part of creating a strategic plan for our lives. Once we have formulated a strategic vision in alignment with our life's purpose, we can then move on to the next step of establishing goals.

TAKE ACTION—*Think and behave as if you have already realized your strategic vision. Then identify the goals required to realize it. Finally, take action to achieve your goals.*

BELIEVE—*Say, "I believe strongly in my strategic vision because I can do anything I set my mind to. I have plenty of talent, and I just need to make sure I develop it through work, focus, and by keeping an open mind so those with the knowledge to do so can help me."*

EMOTIONALIZE—*Consider how it feels having attained the goals in your strategic vision. What kind of person are you and will you become? How will this impact your family and friends?*

COMMIT AND REINFORCE—*Say, "I will achieve my strategic vision no matter what happens." Write a positive affirmation of your strategic vision that contains both a time line and success measurements, and review it daily.*

VISUALIZE—*Imagine being admitted into a college with a high-level basketball program, then being selected for the Olympic team, and finally becoming a professional basketball player.*

Figure 16.2 DETERMINING AND REALIZING A STRATEGIC VISION

Key Points

1. What is a strategic vision?

A picture of desirable circumstances you hope to manifest by following a strategic plan.

2. Why is developing a strategic vision important?

It provides the image of how to fulfill your life's purpose, allowing you to develop goals that act as yardsticks to measure your progress.

3. What is a method for determining and realizing your strategic vision?

Through visualizing, committing and reinforcing, emotionalizing, believing, and actualizing.

Chapter 17

ESTABLISHING GOALS

*There is no hope of success for the person who does not have
a central purpose or definite goal at which to aim.*

—NAPOLEON HILL

The second component of a strategic plan is establishing goals. In doing this, we must keep in mind both our life's purpose and our strategic vision. Many people do not set goals, either because they fear failure or rejection or because they think setting goals is not important. However, setting goals greatly increases our chances for success. Without goals, we remain unfocused, never realizing our strategic vision. With goals, we increase our confidence, develop our competence, boost motivation, and maintain a focus to make our strategic vision a reality.

The information on goal setting in this chapter adapts the excellent model outlined by Brian Tracy in his books *Goals!* and *Flight Plan* to the cultivation of an empowerment mindset as outlined in this book. It also highlights specific steps employed in programming the subconscious mind as discussed in chapter 8.

In *Flight Plan*, Tracy suggests that we define a goal both qualitatively and quantitatively:

◆ *Qualitatively.* Visualize, believe, and emotionalize. You determine how you will think and feel as the result of having achieved a specific goal. You imagine the feeling of pride, satisfaction, joy, happiness, love, peace, and pleasure that you would have if you achieved the perfect goal for you, as you have defined it. You create those feelings within yourself by imagining you have already achieved the goal.

◆ *Quantitatively.* Commit and reinforce, and take action. You define this by attaching specific numbers to it. This gives you a target to aim at and allows you to track progress. If you cannot measure it, you cannot manage it.[1]

Guidelines for setting goals recommended by Tracy, integrated with those in this book for discovering our life's purpose and determining a strategic vision, appear in figure 17.1. To derive the most benefit from these guidelines, write them down and refine the answers throughout the goal-setting process.

Identifying Our Goals

Our goals can only be reached through a vehicle of a plan, in which
we must fervently believe, and upon which we must vigorously act.
There is no other route to success.

—STEPHEN A. BRENNAN

Brian Tracy proposes a simple four-step process that we can use to quickly identify our most important goal and accomplish it quickly. He calls this the "major definite purpose,"[2] but I prefer to call it the "primary goal" to avoid confusion with our life's purpose. This information can be used to refine our strategic vision. For purposes here, I have broken down his suggestions into six steps connecting these to the programming steps for imprinting the goal on the subconscious mind. These steps force us to think with clarity about goals, seeing things we should or should not do to ensure our success.

Step One: Use the Ten-Goal Method
(Visualize, and Commit and Reinforce)

Take a clean sheet of paper and write the word *Goals* and the date at the top. Being mindful of your life's purpose and strategic vision, write down ten goals you would like to accomplish, imagining that you have no limitations of any kind. Write down ten things you would like

GUIDELINES FOR SETTING GOALS

1. Based on your strategic vision, decide exactly what you want in each area of your life. Be specific. Define your goals so clearly that a child could understand them and explain them to another child. *Visualize.*

2. Write down your goals and make them measurable. Goals that are not in writing are merely wishes with no energy behind them. In making them measurable, you create clear targets to aim at. *Commit and reinforce, and take action.*

3. Set a deadline. Be absolutely clear about when you want to achieve each goal. Your subconscious mind loves deadlines; they activate your mental powers and drive you forward. *Emotionalize and believe.*

4. Identify all the obstacles you will have to overcome to achieve your goals. What could possibly go wrong? What stands between you and your goals? What is holding you back or could hold you back? *Visualize and take action.*

5. Determine additional knowledge and skills that you will require to achieve your goals. Remember, whatever got you to where you are today is not enough to get you any further. Every new goal requires the acquisition and application of a new piece of knowledge or a new skill. What are these for you? *Visualize.*

6. Determine whose help and cooperation you will require to achieve your goals. To accomplish large goals, you will need the help of many people. The greater the clarity you have about who those people are, the more likely it is that you will take the steps necessary to gain their cooperation and support. *Visualize.*

7. Make a list of all of your answers to the above questions and organize them by sequence and priority. What do you need to do first? What is most important? A list of activities organized by sequence and priority is a plan, a step-by-step series of tasks that lead you inevitably toward your goals. *Commit and reinforce.*

Figure 17.1

to be, to have, and to do in the future as if each one is guaranteed to happen. To do this, follow Brian Tracy's guidelines summarized in figure 17.2.

Step Two: Select Your Primary Goal
(Visualize and Take Action)

Now ask yourself this question: If I could achieve it right now, what one goal on this list would have the greatest positive impact on my life? Circle that goal. This now becomes your primary goal and the most important destination for the next leg of your life's journey.

Step Three: Make a Plan
(Visualize)

Transfer the goal to the top of a clean sheet of paper. Be sure to write it in the present, positive, personal tense—describing it exactly as if you had already attained it—and set a deadline for its completion. Make a list of difficulties you will have to overcome, the additional information and skill(s) you will require, and the people whose cooper-

GUIDELINES FOR WRITING DOWN SPECIFIC GOALS

1. Write in the present tense, as though your goal has already been achieved. Instead of writing, "I will earn $xxx each year," write, " I earn $xxx each year." Your subconscious mind can only register commands that are phrased in the present tense.

2. Write in the positive tense. Instead of writing, "I will quit smoking," write, "I am a nonsmoker."

3. Write in the personal tense. For this exercise, and for the rest of your life, begin each goal with the word *I* so it is immediately accepted by your subconscious mind as an important command coming down from the "head office."

Figure 17.2

ation you will need to achieve this goal. Organize this information into a plan and take action immediately to begin moving toward your destination.

Step Four: Practice Mindstorming about Your Goal
(Visualize, Commit and Reinforce, and Take Action)

Mindstorming is the process of concentrating intensely on how to achieve your goal. On the top of a clean sheet of paper, write your primary purpose in the form of a question. For example, if your goal was financial, you could write, "How can I earn $xxx by December 31, 20xx?" Then discipline yourself to write at least twenty answers to this question. Your first three to five answers will be fairly simple. You will write that you could do more of this or less of that. The next five answers will be more difficult and will require greater creativity. The last ten answers will require intense concentration and discipline. You will have to dig deep into the resources of your creative mind—and your list of dependable contacts—to reach your goal of twenty answers.

Once you have generated twenty answers, select one and take action on it immediately. This is very important. When you take action on one of these ideas, you tap into your inborn reserves of creativity. There is a direct correlation between how quickly you take action on a new idea and how likely it is that you will ever take action on any new ideas in the future.

Step Five: Project Forward
(Visualize, Emotionalize, and Believe)

Project forward in your mind to the deadline for achieving your goal, imagining that everything worked out, happened on schedule, and the goal was reached. Then look back from the future perspective to where you are today and complete this sentence with twenty answers: "I achieved this goal because I…" Write down everything you could have done to ensure that you were successful. Next, take another sheet of paper and complete this sentence with ten to twenty answers: "I failed to achieve my goal because I didn't…" Make a list of everything you could have done but failed to do that caused you not to achieve your goal.

Step Six: Create a Positive Affirmation
(Commit and Reinforce, Emotionalize, and Believe)

Create a positive affirmation for your primary goal: "My primary goal is to earn $xxx by December 31 by drawing on my ability to focus, work hard, and persevere." This creates a clear mental picture of how your life will be different when you achieve your goal, how you will feel when you achieve it, and all the reasons why you want to achieve it.[3]

When we have achieved our primary goal, we can repeat this process to identify and execute our next primary goal and then our subsequent one, to fulfill further elements of our strategic vision. Once we set the process of establishing our goals in motion, we need to keep moving forward. We should resolve to do something every day that helps us move in the direction of achieving our goals, always believing that we cannot fail.

Key Points

1. **Why are goals important?**

   Because they provide targets for achievement while increasing your confidence, developing your competence, and boosting your motivation.

2. **Why is it important to define goals both qualitatively and quantitatively?**

   Because it helps you to determine how you will think and feel as a result of having achieved particular goals (qualitative), and it provides targets at which to aim and allows you to track your progress (quantitative).

3. **How is a primary goal identified and accomplished?**

   Through using the ten-goal method, selecting your primary goal, making a plan, practicing mindstorming about your goal, projecting forward, and creating a positive affirmation for your goal.

Chapter 18

MAKING A STRATEGIC PLAN

Four steps to achievement:
Plan purposefully.
Prepare prayerfully.
Proceed positively.
Pursue persistently.

—WILLIAM ARTHUR WARD

Now that we have reviewed the various components of a strategic plan, let us address the step-by-step process of making such a plan.

Figure 18.1 illustrates the relationship between our life's purpose, which does not change; our strategic vision, which evolves with time; and goals, which flow from our strategic vision. The goal that would have the greatest positive and most immediate impact on our lives is called our primary goal.

The necessary steps for determining components of a strategic plan are listed in figure 18.2. Once we have reached our primary goal, we can repeat this process to determine our next primary goal to fulfill more elements of our strategic vision.

When making a strategic plan, it is important to put heart and soul into it, as it is the first step toward what we intend to manifest as our new reality of success. Developing a strategic plan according to the process outlined in this book is likely to take considerable time and attention. However, we can be assured that once we have undergone the process we will be well on our way to embracing the empowerment mindset and achieving the goals set out in our strategic plans.

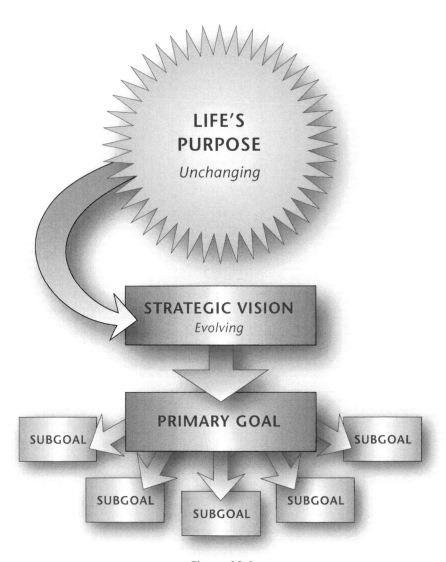

Figure 18.1
KEY ELEMENT OF THE EMPOWERMENT MINDSET EXPRESSED
THROUGH SUBGOALS

LIFE'S PURPOSE
Why you are doing what you most love to do
(unchanging)

1. List two of your unique personal qualities, such as *enthusiasm* and *creativity*.

2. List one or two ways you enjoy expressing those qualities when interacting with others, such as *supporting* and *inspiring*.

3. Describe, in the present tense, the perfect world as you see it and feel it. What does the world look like? How is everyone interacting? What does it feel like?

4. Combine answers one, two, and three into a single statement.

STRATEGIC VISION STATEMENT
What you are doing to express your life's purpose
(changes over time)

1. List five or six personal values.

2. List your passions, dreams, needs, and strengths.

3. Write your strategic vision statement using the preceding information. Write in the first person about the future you wish. Be specific about the goals you want to achieve and give time frames for their achievements, articulating statements in such a way that goals can be evaluated and measured.

Figure 18.2
FINDING OUR LIFE'S PURPOSE AND
CREATING OUR STRATEGIC VISION STATEMENT

STEPS TO MAKING A STRATEGIC PLAN

In cultivating an empowerment mindset, the exercise of making a strategic plan can, on its own, generate profound effects by programming the subconscious mind to achieve goals. Although making a strategic plan may at first look like a lot of work, when broken down into individual steps it is manageable for anyone, as can be seen in the following two scenarios. The procedures used by the two very different individuals in these scenarios can serve as a guide in creating your own strategic plan by writing everything out on lined paper with a pencil as they did.

Scenario One: Darrien

Darrien is a twenty-three-year-old African American, and although he loves learning he has yet to complete twelfth grade. He was brought up in a slum, but his father taught him to enjoy sports and the value of good manners, hard work, and helping others.

Darrien loves the construction industry and wants to one day own his own construction business, as well as have a family. However, currently he is stuck in low-paying, labor-intensive jobs that never lead to anything better. And the harder he tries to improve his life, the more peer pressure he feels from his friends not to be "uppity" and to accept life in the slum, from which they feel they have no escape. Darrien's younger sister has already had a baby, but the father has deserted her. His brother was killed in gang violence, and his father passed away of natural causes several years ago. But despite his difficult circumstances, Darrien is determined to create a better life for his mother, sister, young nephew, and himself. He begins by developing a strategic plan, breaking down the work required into the steps that follow.

Step 1: Darrien Discovers His Life's Purpose

Darrien takes a blank sheet of lined paper and, preparing to discover his life's purpose, writes the date at the top, leaving space to record any future dates on which he might revise his life's purpose, knowing it may evolve over time due to new circumstances or increased understanding. As he begins to write, he keeps in mind that his life's purpose explains why he chooses what he does and is intended to reflect what he is good at and brings him the greatest joy.

He hopes to discover his life's purpose in one sitting but will not worry if he does not express it exactly right during his first attempt. He realizes the importance of just getting something on paper so he becomes committed to the task. The process allows Darrien to visualize and emotionalize his life's purpose more precisely.

The results of Darrien's efforts follow.

Step 1

April 2, 2012
Revised on the following dates:

_____

_____

_____

1) Two of my unique personal qualities are persistence and hope.

2) I enjoy expressing the qualities by being hardworking and encouraging when interacting with others.

3) The perfect world as I see and feel it is one where:

People feel secure enough to cooperate with one another to reach their individual and collective goals. The world is a safe place. Families and communities are organized with a common purpose. Everyone can see the opportunities that exist, and people also understand what they need to do to take advantage of those opportunities.

4) Combining the three prior points into a single statement,

My life's purpose is:

_____

Through hard work and encouragement, to demonstrate to African Americans how they might, with persistence and hope, establish a secure world of opportunity through understanding, cooperation, commitment, and knowledge.

Step 2: Darrien Determines His Strategic Vision

Darrien takes a blank sheet of lined paper and, preparing to determine his strategic vision, writes the date at the top, leaving space to record any future dates on which he might revise his strategic vision. As he begins to write, he keeps in mind that his strategic vision explains what he chooses to do with his life and is the strategy behind how he expresses his life's purpose.

He seeks to determine his strategic vision in one sitting but will not worry if he does not express it exactly right during his first attempt. He realizes it is important just to get something on paper so he becomes committed to the task. The process allows Darrien to visualize and emotionalize his strategic vision more precisely.

The results of Darrien's efforts follow.

Step 2

April 2, 2012
Revised on the following dates:

_____

_____

_____

1) The six personal values I subscribe to are: tolerance, generosity, trust, integrity, restraint, and cooperation.

2) My passions, dreams, needs, and strengths are as follows:

Passions: I love my family. I love to learn, and I like building things. I love sports, especially basketball and football. I like helping people who appreciate my efforts.

Dreams: I dream of finishing my high school education and either going to a trade school to learn carpentry or getting a degree in construction-related engineering. I dream of creating a safe environment for my mother, sister, and nephew so that they are happy and can realize their highest potential. I dream of eventually owning my own construction company so that I can be in charge of my life and provide more opportunities for myself and my family. I dream of being able to have a family with a good woman, bring up our family in a secure environment, and offer our children advantages that I never had. I dream of being able to show the world what neighborhoods and communities can realize if they develop a common vision for a better future and cooperate against all odds to grasp it.

Needs: To achieve my dreams, I need to finish twelfth grade, then I need to go either to trade school or university. I need more income and better employment circumstances to create a safer environment for my family.

Strengths: My strengths are: I am hardworking, persistent, kind, supportive, committed to making a better life, love learning, and know what it is like to grow up in a harsh environment.

3) [I write my strategic vision statement using the preceding information. I write in the first person and describe the future I wish for. I am specific, set the goals I want to achieve, give a time frame, and artic-ulate the statements in such a way that they can be evaluated and measured.]

My strategic vision is:

Relying on my integrity, ability to cooperate, tolerance, toughness, and ability to work hard, I will create a more secure environment for my family by completing my education and putting myself in a position where I can earn more income to realize such opportunities. I will com-plete requirements for the twelfth grade within six months. I will find a higher paying construction job within one year. I will find a more secure environment for my family within two years. I will finish a carpenter's certification within three years or a degree in construction-related engineering within five years. I will establish a profitable construction business within ten years.

Darrien takes a blank sheet of lined paper and, preparing to establish ten goals, writes the date at the top, leaving space to record any future dates on which he might revise his goals. As he starts writing, he recalls that his goals reflect how he chooses to implement his strategic vision. After writing his ten goals, he selects his primary goal.

He seeks to establish his goals in one sitting but knows that it might take longer since much detail is required. He won't worry if they are not expressed exactly right during his first attempt. He realizes it is important just to get something on paper so he becomes committed to the task. The process of doing this allows Darrien to begin to emotionalize and visualize more precisely what his goals might be.

The results of Darrien's efforts follow.

Step 3

April 2, 2012
Revised on the following dates:

_____
_____

_____

My Goals

1) *I graduate from twelfth grade within six months.*

2) *I am earning $30,000 annually from a construction job within one year.*

3) *I am in a more secure neighborhood with better schools with my mother, sister, and nephew within two years.*

4) *I am a certified carpenter within three years.*

5) *I am a construction engineer within five years.*

6) *I own a profitable construction business within ten years.*

7) I am married within seven years.

8) I own my own home within twenty years.

9) I am able to provide my children with a good education so they can graduate and go on to advanced training or education within twenty years.

10) I establish a society to help African Americans escape slums within twenty-five years.

[I have selected the following as my primary goal because it is the goal that, if I could achieve it right now, would have the greatest positive impact on my life since it is a prerequisite for many of my other goals.]

My primary goal is:

I graduate from twelfth grade within six months.

Step 4: Darrien Focuses on His Primary Goal

Darrien takes a blank sheet of lined paper and writes the date at the top, leaving space to record any future dates on which he might revise this document. Next he writes at the top "Darrien's Primary Goal" and enters it in the line below. He then describes his primary goal as if he had already attained it, sets a deadline for its completion, and lists the difficulties he must overcome, the information and skills needed, and the people whose cooperation is essential to achieving his goal.

He seeks to come up with this information in one sitting but knows that it may take longer since much detail is required. He won't worry if he cannot record all the information exactly right during his first attempt. He realizes that it is important just to get something on paper so he becomes committed to detailing the information. The process allows Darrien to visualize and emotionalize his primary goal more precisely.

The results of Darrien's efforts follow.

Step 4

Darrien's Primary Goals

I graduate from twelfth grade within six months.

1) I feel like I have accomplished something that has eluded every member of my family. It may not seem like much to middle-class white people, but it is an enormous hurdle for someone from a slum environment. It feels really good to have done this. My mother and sister are proud of me. But I know I can do more. I am now in a position to get a higher-paying construction job to pursue some of my other dreams. Most importantly, it is the first step to finding a healthier living environment for my family and for reaching my other goals.

2) My deadline for completing twelfth grade is six months.

3) The difficulties I must overcome are:

a. Peer pressure from my friends to quit

b. Poor study habits

c. Time challenges from both attending night school and working full-time

d. Social disruption challenges from neighborhood upheavals

e. Fatigue from working during the day and going to school at night

f. Cost of the night school course

g. Time away from family

h. Unfamiliarity with school environment

i. Rusty skills in the three Rs

j. Fear of failing

k. Concerns about racism

4) The information and skills I require are:

a. I need to contact my old high school and obtain transcripts of my school records and a summary of twelfth grade courses completed and those that are required to graduate.

b. Once I determine the courses I need to finish, I must contact various colleges and night schools to find out:

i. Which offers the most appropriate program for my interests in terms of cost, location, and availability

ii. The availability of secondhand textbooks for the courses I require

c. I need to confirm with my employer that my time at work will not interfere with night classes.

d. I need to contact counselors at educational institutions or in government social service agencies to determine if there are any loans, scholarship possibilities, or other forms of sponsorship for course costs, transportation, and so forth.

e. I must contact various government and educational agencies and explore what help might be provided for course costs, transportation, and so forth.

f. In light of my larger goals of carpenter certification or obtaining a university degree, I should investigate what computer or math courses are available and may be taken at the same time.

g. I should investigate whether there are African American study groups or volunteer tutors at the educational institution.

5) People whose cooperation is essential for achieving my goal are:

a. *Family—I need to explain my plans for attaining my primary goal to my mother and sister and hopefully gain their support for my short- and long-term plans.*

b. *Employer—I need to talk to my employer to establish that my job will not interfere with my night school and study requirements.*

c. *Friends—I need to tell friends about my plans, how serious I am about them, and that until I complete twelfth grade requirements I am off limits socially.*

d. *Church minister—I need to talk to my church minister to see if any assistance may be available in the form of tutoring or money to offset course costs.*

e. *Government and educational agencies—I should contact various government and educational agencies to explore what help might be provided for course costs, transportation, and so forth.*

Step 5: Darrien Organizes Information into a Strategic Plan

Darrien takes a blank sheet of lined paper and writes the date at the top, leaving space to record any future dates on which he might revise this document. Next he writes at the top "Strategic Plan." He then prioritizes and describes in detail important parts of the plan he needs to address, including the collection of information, evaluation and advance decisions, organizations, and preparation. After completing this list of measurable tasks, he takes action immediately to implement the plan.

Although Darrien seeks to provide this information in one sitting, he understands that it may take longer to think through all the necessary details. He won't worry if they are not expressed exactly right during his first attempt since revision is expected. The process allows Darrien to visualize and emotionalize his personal strategic plan.

The results of Darrien's efforts follow.

Step 5

April 2, 2012
Revised on the following dates:

_____

_____

_____

Strategic Plan

1) Day 1: Collection of critical information — In the following order, I:

a. Contact local colleges and night schools to learn:

i. Which offers the most appropriate night school program for completing the twelfth grade courses needed to graduate.

ii. The start and finish time of the program and associated costs.

iii. The location of the institution and its proximity to public transportation.

iv. The availability of financial assistance and application deadlines.

v. Whether there are African American study groups or volunteer tutors.

b. Contact local church minister to inquire if any assistance might be provided by the church or its members in the form of tutoring or money to offset course costs.

2) Day 2: Evaluation and advance decisions — In the following order, with a clear idea of when I will start night courses (and the costs involved), I:

a. DECISION POINT: Decide on educational institution and submit application to it.

b. Advise my family and employer of my plans.

3) Day 3: Advance organization and preparation — In the following order, I:

a. Organize, prepare, and send applications for potential subsidies/low-income educational support.

b. Investigate what computer or math courses are available at the institution I might attend and whether they can be taken concurrently with the twelfth grade courses.

4) Day X: Major decisions – After response to college night school application arrives, with start date in mind and in the following order, I:

a. Advise family and employer of start date.

b. Make up daily/weekly/monthly course schedule.

c. Investigate best public transit route to educational institution.

d. Contact educational institution bookstore for advice on where best to find used textbooks.

e. DECISION POINT: Decide whether to enroll in additional courses and submit application.

5) Day X + I:

a. Contact organizer of educational institution study group for African American students and inquire about meeting times and whether volunteer tutors are available.

b. Advise church minister of plan and follow up with any tutorial/financial assistance that might be available.

Step 6: Darrien Mindstorms

Darrien takes a blank sheet of lined paper and writes the date at the top, leaving space to record any future dates on which he might revise this document. Next he writes at the top of the page his primary goal in the form of a question. He then writes twenty answers to this question, reflecting ways to achieve his primary goal. After reviewing all twenty answers, he decides to take action on number two since he can do it immediately, its cost is not too high, and he thinks the structured environment would help him achieve his goal.

The results of Darrien's efforts follow.

Step 6

April 2, 2012
Revised on the following dates:

_____

_____

_____

How can I finish twelfth grade in six months?

I can:

1) Quit my job and focus completely on finishing twelfth grade.

2) Take night school courses.

3) Take an online course.

4) Take a correspondence course.

5) Ask my church to sponsor me.

6) Ask my church parishioners if they can help me find a sponsor.

7) Ask my church if they can help me find a higher-paying job.

8) Work on weekends to earn extra money.

9) Find an individual patron to sponsor me.

10) Find a corporate patron to sponsor me.

11) See if my current employer might consider sponsoring me.

12) Try to find a construction company that would sponsor me (especially if there is one owned by an African American).

13) Borrow a modest amount from friends and relatives.

14) Borrow books from the library, enroll in courses on my own time, and take government exams.

15) Borrow books from the library, enroll in courses on my own time, and study with a tutor before taking government exams.

16) Panhandle on weekends with an innovative pamphlet that explains what I am trying to do.

17) Organize fifty/fifty nightly rap, dancing, or basketball competitions in the neighborhood as fundraisers, with half the proceeds going to the winners and half to my educational charity.

18) Borrow books from my old high school with sample exams and do a self-study course.

19) Ask my old schoolteachers if they could provide course material and advice so that I can pass the exams.

20) Appeal to a local college or university for a student to mentor me.

Step 7: Darrien Projects Forward

Darrien takes a blank sheet of lined paper and writes the date at the top, leaving space to record any future dates on which he might revise this document. Next he writes at the top of the page what it feels like to have reached his primary goal, including how people now see and react to him. This process helps him visualize, emotionalize, and actualize reaching the goal.

Then for further clarity he writes twenty reasons why he achieved the goal, fifteen steps he took to successfully reach it, and fifteen reasons for failing to reach it, as well as listing everything he could have done but failed to do that kept him from reaching the goal. Finally, he creates a positive affirmation for his primary goal, understanding that it provides a clear mental picture of how his life will be different when he achieves the goal.

The results of Darrien's efforts follow.

Step 7

1) I have achieved my primary goal by my deadline. It appeared to be a big challenge when I started, given my circumstances, but I overcame my difficulties. I am proud to be the first person in my family to have finished high school. Even though my friends think I am "uppity" for trying to improve my life, I know they also have more respect for me because I have achieved something that few people in our neighborhood have. My mother and sister are also proud of me. Now I am motivated and more confident about reaching my larger goals.

2) I achieved this goal because:

a. I withstood pressure from my friends who wanted me to quit.

b. I wanted to set a good example for my younger sister and other youth in the neighborhood.

c. Having it made me feel more confident.

d. I wanted to demonstrate that I could achieve what I want by putting my heart and mind to it.

e. I wanted to apply to trade school or a college or university.

f. I wanted to earn more money.

g. I like to learn and am persistent.

h. I wanted to have more choices in my life.

i. I wanted to prove to myself, my friends, and the church minister that I could finish what I set out to accomplish.

j. I believed in myself.

k. I wanted to challenge myself.

l. It provided an easy way of getting back into education, which will be valuable for achieving other goals

m. It allowed me to get out of my neighborhood so I could intermingle with people who have a broader perspective.

n. I kept focusing on it and was not distracted by socializing with friends.

o. I found sufficient financial support.

p. I wanted to be respected.

q. I had the right values and attitudes.

r. I wanted to own a construction business.

s. I wanted to have a better life for myself and family than my father could provide.

t. I wanted to provide a future wife and children with options for a better life.

3) I did the following to ensure that I was successful in reaching this goal:

a. Reached out and sought the help of other people.

b. Kept an eye on my long-term goals.

c. Constantly thought about the unsafe slum environment where I live.

d. Ignored the criticisms and pressure from my neighborhood friends.

e. Prepared a thorough strategic plan and followed it.

f. Organized the resources and people in my life so I could do it.

g. Was absolutely committed to achieving it.

h. Had sufficient self-confidence.

i. Had the self-discipline to stay on my chosen path.

j. Never thought about giving up, due to my quality of persistence.

k. "Rolled with the punches," so that adverse circumstances did not discourage me from my path.

l. Advised my family, friends, employer, and church minister of my goal and got their support.

m. Was prepared to take any action necessary.

n. Worked hard to produce results.

o. Got inspiration from other people in the educational institution and my local church.

4) I failed to achieve this goal because I didn't:

a. Withstand peer pressure and gave up.

b. Prepare a strategic plan.

c. Have sufficient self-confidence to stand up against the odds of failure.

d. Believe in myself.

e. Take it seriously.

f. Put the effort into doing the work.

g. Focus on it sufficiently.

h. Raise the money for the course and transportation.

i. Reorganize my life around achieving the goal.

j. Bring the right values to the task.

k. Relax enough to learn.

l. Prepare well enough for schoolwork and develop good enough study habits.

m. Have a good attitude.

n. Get support from my employer.

o. Realize my mother, sister, and nephew would be a distraction.

5) Everything I could have done but failed to do to that kept me from reaching my goal is:

a. Take it more seriously.

b. Work harder.

c. Prepare better.

d. Focus more intently.

e. Undertake detailed research.

f. Communicate better with all parties involved in my achieving this goal.

g. Believe in myself and bring the right attitude and values to the task.

6) My positive affirmation for my primary goal is:

My primary goal is to complete twelfth grade in six months because I know I have the ability, discipline, and power to do anything I focus on and set my mind to.

Scenario Two: Connie

Connie is a thirty-five-year-old single mother with two children, ages eight and ten. She has a job just above entry level, is earning $30,000 annually, and also has some equity in a modest duplex. She struggles financially and believes her financial literacy and budgeting skills are inadequate. She married after finishing only her second year of college and feels she has hit a ceiling in her ability to earn more, which is holding her back professionally and preventing her from being able to offer better educational opportunities and an improved quality of life for her children.

Connie is a running enthusiast and loves teaching children. Since her children are young, she has very little time to socialize or pursue her hobby as an artist. But despite her limited skills and her family obligations Connie is determined to create a better life for her children and herself.

She begins by developing a strategic plan, breaking down the work required into the steps that follow.

Step 1: Connie Discovers Her Life's Purpose

Connie takes a blank sheet of lined paper and, preparing to discover her life's purpose, writes the date at the top, leaving space to record any future dates on which she might revise her life's purpose, knowing it may evolve over time due to new circumstances or increased understanding. As she begins to write, she keeps in mind that her life's purpose explains why she chooses what she does and is intended to reflect what she is good at and brings her the greatest joy.

She seeks to discover her life's purpose in one sitting but will not worry if she does not express it exactly right during her first attempt. She realizes it is important just to get something on paper so she becomes more committed to the task. The process allows Connie to visualize and emotionalize her life's purpose more precisely.

The results of Connie's efforts follow.

Step 1

April 2, 2012
Revised on the following dates:

_____

_____

_____

1) Two of my unique personal qualities are positivity and creativity.

2) I enjoy expressing these qualities by being supportive and inspiring when interacting with others.

3) The perfect world as I see and feel it is one where:
People feel secure and confident. Everyone is satisfied and happy with their lot in life. People have hope because they feel they are valuable contributing members of a community and so are part of something larger than themselves.

4) Combining the three prior points into a single statement,

My life's purpose is:

To use my creativity and enthusiasm to educate and inspire others so they can feel secure, confident, satisfied, and happy; become valued for their contributions to the community; and feel they are a part of something larger than themselves.

Step 2: Connie Determines Her Strategic Vision

Connie takes a blank sheet of lined paper and, preparing to determine her strategic vision, writes the date at the top, leaving space to record any future dates on which she might revise her strategic vision. As she begins to write, she keeps in mind that her strategic vision explains what she chooses to do with her life and it is the strategy behind how she expresses her life's purpose.

She seeks to determine her strategic vision in one sitting but will not worry if she does not express it exactly right during her first attempt. She realizes that it is important just to get something on paper so she becomes more committed to the task. The process allows Connie to visualize and emotionalize her strategic vision more precisely.

The results of Connie's efforts follow.

Step 2

April 2, 2012
Revised on the following dates:

_____

_____

_____

1) The six personal values I subscribe to are: honesty, perseverance, passion, trust, kindness, and gratitude.

2) My passions, dreams, needs, and strengths are as follows:

Passions: I love my children and my family. I love to teach children and to paint. I also love to run for exercise.

Dreams: I dream of finishing my education so I can say I have obtained a degree in a discipline. I dream of having more time for my family and doing the things I love. I dream of establishing a successful business and career out of the things I like to do. I dream of running a marathon.

Needs: To achieve my dreams, I need the time and resources to obtain a degree. I need more income and better employment circumstances so that I can spend more time with my children and do the things I love. Strengths: My strengths are: I am hardworking, open-minded, empathetic, and readily adapt to new situations.

3) [I write my strategic vision statement using the preceding information. I write in the first person and describe the future I wish. I am specific, set the goals I want to achieve, give a time frame, and articulate the statements in such a way that they can be evaluated and measured.]

My strategic vision is:

Relying on my values and strengths, I will fulfill my passions and dreams. I will run a full marathon within one year. I will spend more quality time with my children within two years. I will graduate with an arts and education degree within two years. I will establish a profitable business teaching children art within six years.

Step 3: Connie Establishes Her Goals

Connie takes a blank sheet of lined paper and writes the date at the top, leaving space to record any future dates on which she might revise her ten goals. As she starts writing, she recalls that her goals set out how she chooses to implement her strategic vision. After writing her ten goals, she selects her primary goal.

Connie seeks to establish her goals in one sitting but knows that it may take longer since much detail is required. She won't worry if they are not expressed exactly right during her first attempt. She realizes that it is important just to get something on paper so she becomes committed to the task. The process allows Connie to visualize and emotionalize her goals more precisely.

The results of Connie's efforts follow.

Step 3

April 2, 2012
Revised on the following dates:

_____

_____

_____

My Goals

1) I run a full marathon with a well-conditioned body within one year.

2) I own a more reliable vehicle within two years.

3) I graduate with an arts and education degree within two years.

4) I have more time to spend with my children within two years.

5) I am happy with a new life partner within three years.

6) I own a profitable business teaching children art within six years.

7) I have earned enough money for my children to have their post-secondary education paid for within nine years.

8) I own a house within fifteen years.

9) I am married within fifteen years.

10) I own a home in an upscale neighborhood within twenty years.

[I have selected the following as my primary goal because it is the goal that, if I could achieve it right now, would have the greatest positive impact on my life since it is a prerequisite for many of my other goals.]

My primary goal is:

I graduate with an arts and education degree within two years.

Step 4: Connie Focuses on Her Primary Goal

Connie takes a blank sheet of lined paper and writes the date at the top, leaving space to record any future dates on which she might revise this document. Next she writes at the top "Connie's Primary Goal" and enters it in the line below. She then describes her primary goal as if she had already attained it, sets a deadline for its completion, and makes a list of the difficulties she must overcome, the information and skills needed, and the people whose cooperation is essential to achieving her goal.

She seeks to come up with this information in one sitting but knows that it may take longer since much detail is required. She won't worry if she cannot record all the information exactly right during her first attempt. She realizes that it is important just to get something on paper so she becomes committed to detailing the information. The process allows Connie to visualize and emotionalize her primary goal more precisely.

The results of Connie's efforts follow.

Step 4

April 2, 2012
Revised on the following dates:

_____

_____

_____

Connie's Primary Goal

I graduate with an arts and education degree within two years.

1) I feel like I have accomplished something that has been "unfinished business" for me. I learned so much about art and education, and educating young children. I am now in a position to secure a higher paying job and develop a new business. I feel more confident and optimistic. I feel people will not look down on me in the workplace for being "lesser" than them. I am motivated to move forward to succeed in my other goals.

2) My deadline for completing the arts and education degree is two years.

3) The difficulties I must overcome are:

a. Weak financial literacy and budgeting skills

b. Education costs

c. Living costs and employment challenges while attending university

d. Moving closer to the educational institution

e. Babysitting costs

f. Time away from my children

g. Past history as a slow learner

h. Rusty technological skills and the need to update computer hardware and software

i. Fear of going back to school and change

j. Potential resistance from children

4) The information and skills I require are:

a. I need to either self-learn financial literacy and budgeting skills or take a crash night or online course.

b. I need to contact local colleges and universities to learn (either speaking to or meeting with a student counselor):

i. Which institution offers the most appropriate degree program for my interests and a detailed list of course requirements.

ii. The costs involved and the availability of student loans.

iii. The start date of the program.

iv. Whether it is possible to take night courses or online courses from my home.

v. The availability of secondhand textbooks for the courses I require.

vi. Whether there is any low-cost housing available for financially strapped single parents.

c. I need to find out what the costs of babysitting services are for the times I attend classes and explore options with family members who live near me.

d. I need to explore options that may help me learn faster, such as speed reading.

e. I should update my computer skills for office software and computer hardware, which may be beneficial for an arts and education degree.

f. I should explore online single-parent groups, blogs, Web sites in my area to inquire how others in my situation are dealing with similar issues.

5) People whose cooperation I require to achieve my goal are:

a. Children—I need to explain to my children the plans I have for attaining my primary goal and how short-term sacrifices need to be made for our long-term well-being.

b. Employer—I need to talk to my employer to see if I can work flex time to accommodate my course schedule or, if it is possible, to secure a higher paying position with some flexibility.

c. Parents—I need to talk to my parents, explain my plans to them and inquire if they can:

i. Provide support for babysitting

ii. Provide educational or other financial support

d. Siblings—I need to talk to my siblings who live close by to see if they can help with babysitting.

e. Friends, close associates, and church minister—I need to talk to my friends, close associates (such as my running group), and church minister to see if any assistance might be gratuitously provided for the difficulties I must overcome.

f. Government agencies—I should contact various government agencies to find out about housing and living subsidies.

g. College or university professors—Once I have decided what college or university I wish to attend and the courses I need to take, I should contact each professor and find out more about the course requirements, explaining my situation and primary goal, and exploring flexible options for a single parent balancing the needs of family and work.

Connie takes a blank sheet of lined paper and writes the date at the top, leaving space to record any future dates on which she might revise this document. Next she writes at the top "Strategic Plan." She then prioritizes and describes in detail important parts of the plan she needs to address, including the collection of information, evaluation, and advance decisions, organization, and reparation. After completing this list of measurable tasks, she takes action immediately to implement the plan.

Although Connie seeks to provide this information in one sitting, she understands that it may take longer to think through all the necessary details. She won't worry if they are not expressed exactly right during her first attempt. The process allows Connie to visualize and emotionalize her personal strategic plan.

The results of Connie's efforts follow.

Step 5

April 2, 2012
Revised on the following dates:

_____

_____

_____

Strategic Plan

1) Week 1: Collection of critical information – In the following order, I:

a. Contact local colleges and universities and meet with student counselors to learn:

i. Which offers the most appropriate degree program

for my interests and a detailed list of course requirements.

    ii. The availability of scholarships, student loans, or grants and costs – application deadlines for each.

    iii. The start date of the programs.

    iv. Whether it is possible to take night courses or online courses from my home.

  b. Investigate self-learning options for financial literacy and budgeting skills or crash night courses or online courses; seek out anything that might be provided for free and evaluate costs of courses that must be paid for.

  c. Gather information on costs of babysitting services for the times I need to attend classes and explore options with parents and siblings who live near me.

2) Weeks 2 and 3: Critical meetings and decisions – In the following order, with a clear idea of when I might start college or university, costs involved, and costs associated with child care, I:

  a. Organize, call, or attend meetings with children, employer, parents, siblings, friends, close associates, church minister, and government agencies to discuss my future plans and possible support – flextime options and related plans.

b. Explore financial subsidy or earning options and evaluate options and time lines most suitable for me.

c. Review cost-cutting measures and the availability of subsidized housing.

d. Investigate options that may help me to learn faster, such as speed reading.

e. Explore and join online single-parent groups – blogs–Web sites in my area to inquire how others in my situation are dealing with similar issues.

f. Decision Point: I decide which option for financial literacy and budgeting skills is best for me and enroll, buy self-help books, and either identify start date or begin immediately.

3) Week 4: Advance organization and preparation – In the following order, I:

a. Organize, prepare, and send application for college – university and establish expected time of acceptance – rejection. I do this with the two or three educational institutions highest on my list so that if one does not accept me there is still the possibility the others will.

b. Organize, prepare, and submit applications for scholarships, student loans, or grants.

c. Organize, prepare, and submit applications for subsidized housing.

d. Implement family cost-cutting measures that can be taken immediately.

e. Evaluate options for updating my computer skills for office software and computer hardware that may be beneficial for an arts degree.

f. Continue training to develop financial literacy and budgeting skills.

4) Week 5: More preparation – In the following order, I:

a. Decision Point: Decide which course training I need to update my computer skills and begin immediately.

b. Make follow-up calls to colleges and universities to ensure applications were received and are being processed and seek expected response times.

5) Week X: Major decisions – After responses to college and university applications come in, in the following order I:

a. Decision Point: Decide which educational institution I will attend.

b. Arrange for the prerequisite courses I need to take and the optional ones I wish to attend.

c. Meet with or contact children, employer, parents, siblings, friends, close associates, church minister, and government agencies to inform

them of my plans and discuss possible support—
flextime options and timeline.

d. Inquire about low-cost housing possibilities for
single parents.

e. <u>Decision Point:</u> Evaluate and accept or reject vari-
ous opportunities for assistance.

f. Make plans to move to new premises and engage
childcare services.

g. Arrange for new employment.

6) <u>Week X + 1:</u>

a. Explain my situation and primary goal to my
future professors and explore alternatives in course
material and deadlines for single parents.

b. Search the bookstore and Internet for secondhand
textbooks.

Step 6: Connie Mindstorms

Connie takes a blank sheet of lined paper and writes the date at the top, leaving space to record any future dates on which she might revise this document. Next she writes at the top of the page her primary goal in the form of a question. She then writes twenty answers to this question, reflecting ways to achieve her primary goal. After reviewing these twenty answers, she decides to take action on number two since she can do that immediately, its cost is not too high, and she thinks the structured environment would help her achieve her goal.

The results of Connie's efforts follow.

Step 6

April 2, 2012

Revised on the following dates:

_____

_____

_____

How can I finish my degree in two years?

I can:

1) Take out a line of credit against my duplex.

2) Take an intensive course load after work.

3) Find employment that allows me flexibility to attend day classes.

4) Borrow money from my parents.

5) Win a scholarship.

6) Win a grant.

7) Get a student loan.

8) Find an individual patron to sponsor me.

9) Find a corporate patron to sponsor me.

10) See if my current employer might consider being my sponsor.

11) Organize a charity lottery, and after the winner takes the cash prize I win my education as a charitable contribution.

12) Make a public appeal for support through the media, promising art lessons to young people in return.

13) Make paintings of wealthy or famous people and auction them off at a charity event, with me receiving 50 percent of the proceeds.

14) Offer my art services to a media outlet as a story in return for a fee.

15) Busk with my art on the weekends in well-heeled, high-traffic areas of the city to collect money.

16) Go door-to-door offering to paint portraits of families, their houses, or their pets for sale.

17) Make a YouTube video with an angle that might attract sales of my art.

18) Approach major giftware providers and see if I can make art for corporate or personal gifts.

19) Teach art classes after work.

20) Approach local business organizations (chamber of commerce, board of trade, rotary club, and so forth) offering to create custom-made artwork for their organization's fundraising efforts.

Step 7: Connie Projects Forward

Connie takes a blank sheet of lined paper and writes the date at the top, leaving space to record any future dates on which she might revise this document. Next she writes at the top of the page what it feels like to have reached her primary goal, including how people now see and react to her. This helps her visualize, emotionalize, and actualize reaching the goal.

Then for further clarity she writes twenty reasons why she achieved the goal, fifteen steps she took to successfully reach the goal, and fifteen reasons for failing to reach it, as well as a list of everything she could have done but failed to do that kept her from reaching her goal. Finally, she creates a positive affirmation for her primary goal, understanding that it provides a clear mental picture of how her life will be different when she achieves the goal.

The results of Connie's efforts follow.

Step 7

April 2, 2012
Revised on the following dates:

_____

_____

_____

1) I have reached my primary goal by the time of my primary deadline. It appeared to be such a big hill to climb when I started from such an impoverished, uneducated position, and I lacked confidence. But I overcame critics and obstacles. Now I don't have to feel inadequate for not attaining something I always thought was important. Just achieving this goal has made me feel more confident—like I can do anything I set my mind to. I am also now in a position to move forward to achieve my other goals and to be able to create more resources to put my family in a better position.

2) I achieved this goal because:

a. Not completing my degree would have left me with a feeling of "unfinished business."

b. I wanted to set a good example for my children and contribute to their futures.

c. I wanted to feel more confident.

d. I was able to study what I love.

e. It was a precursor for me to earn more money.

f. I knew it would allow me more choices in life.

g. I had sufficient self-confidence.

h. I wanted to show my parents and siblings that I could finish what I started.

i. I confided in family and friends so they were understanding about my schedule.

j. I wanted to challenge myself.

k. It allowed me to get out of the house and meet interesting people who gave me support.

l. I got information from blogs written by others in similar situations.

m. I enjoyed learning new things.

n. My former husband belittled my abilities and discouraged me from trying anything challenging.

o. I was able to find sufficient financial help.

p. I didn't want fellow workers looking down on me for my lack of education.

q. It brought me closer to what I love to do— teach art to children.

r. It allowed me to address some of my deficiencies as a person.

s. I knew it would help me move constructively forward with my life.

t. I wanted to develop my own creativity through studying art.

3) I did the following to ensure that I was successful in reaching this goal:

a. Prepared a thorough strategic plan and followed it.

b. Organized the finances and the logistics of my life so I could do it.

c. Committed to achieving it.

d. Focused on achieving it.

e. Had the self-discipline to stay on my chosen path.

f. Never entertained the notion of giving up at any stage or allowed anyone to discourage me..

g. Was prepared to adapt to any situation without losing focus on my goal.

h. Communicated clearly to everyone whose support and advice I needed.

i. Never hesitated to take necessary action.

j. Never let my energy flag in getting the work done.

k. Sought the necessary help of other people.

l. Knew I could overcome any obstacle to my goal no matter how formidable.

m. Ensured that I never neglected my children, so I didn't feel guilty.

n. Overcame my fear of failure.

o. Budgeted wisely and obtained necessary financial help.

4) I failed to achieve this goal because I didn't:

a. Prepare a strategic plan.

b. Believe in myself.

c. Have a 100 percent commitment to it.

d. Understand the difficulty of doing it.

e. Have the self-discipline to do the little things necessary to accomplish the big things.

f. Have the ability to raise necessary finances.

g. Reorganize my life so I could pursue it.

h. Keep myself from becoming discouraged by other people.

i. Maintain my focus.

j. Approach my goal with enough energy.

k. Have a good attitude.

l. Have the best values to accomplish it.

m. Realize my children could be so much of a distraction.

n. Get the support of my employer.

5) Everything I could have done but failed to that kept me from reaching my goal is:

a. Prepare myself better to anticipate the obstacles and challenges I encountered.

b. Budget more wisely.

c. Communicate more clearly to get the support of the key people I needed to succeed.

d. Take more seriously the necessity of preparing a detailed strategic plan.

e. Convince myself that I could succeed, to keep my energy and attitude in better form.

f. Not hesitate to take action when it was required.

g. More accurately assess the workload involved in taking courses, holding a job, and looking after my family.

6) My positive affirmation for my primary goal is:

My primary goal is to complete my arts and

education degree in two years because I know I have
unlimited power and ability to achieve anything.

Although this process may seem somewhat tedious, if followed diligently and sincerely it will produce successful results. It is far better to spend a little focused time creating a strategic plan that will set us on a path to achievement than to regret a lifetime of failure.

By creating our own strategic plans through following the steps taken by Darrien or Connie, we will be well on our way to reaching the primary goal of our strategic vision. Then we can continue to use the same process to achieve the various other goals of our strategic vision. Once we have achieved a few of these goals, our confidence will grow along with our happiness as we come closer to fulfilling our life's purpose.

Learning with Grandpa

LITTLE BOY'S WORLD

Grandpa's world, kind and warm
Ocean placid, seldom storm.

Uncle's world, gray and mean
In decay, never green.

Grandpa's view, acting right
Keeping focus, goals in sight.

Cousin struggles, world at war
Baby steps, not going far.

Grandpa's bearing, much content
Negative notions, pay no rent.

Father stands, stooped and sad
Mighty weight, seldom glad.

Grandpa's insight, life unfair
Powerful worry, undue wear.

Auntie's anxious, fretting sort
Life a cancer, not a wart.

Grandpa never, himself first
Tiptop manners, avoiding worst.

Neighbor's daughter, great conceit

New age blinder, self-defeat.

Grandpa's credo, work to heart

Endless talk, never start.

Sister's life, nonstop play

Leaving effort, others to pay.

Grandpa's center, path ahead

Life a flower, fear to shed.

All people, you and me

Each with power, destiny.

Whole picture, truly see

Wisdom's effort, set you free.

All people, me and you

To be like Grandpa—through and through.

CONCLUSION

The Empowerment Mindset As a Way of Life

My greatest challenge has been to change the mindsets of people. Mindsets play strange tricks on us. We see things the way our minds have instructed our eyes to see.

—MUHAMMAD YUNUS

Once we have understood and adopted the various aspects of the empowerment mindset, it is beneficial to make these practices part of our daily lives to maintain them. To overcome the WSC syndrome and habitual failure, it is critical to keep appreciating how our empowerment mindset contributes to our success and happiness. Our negative emotions and toxic thoughts lead to defeatist attitudes that can manifest as learned helplessness; a victim mentality; self-pity; lateral violence; fear; depression; and, in some circumstances, community- or group-conditioned negative thinking. It is also important to recognize the negative impact of having an inflated ego and how perceiving reality as static traps us in our comfort zones.

To transform ourselves, we must embrace an open mind of reinvention, realizing that education is part of the process of ongoing growth that requires adaptation to changing situations. In addition, to unlock our potential we need to be aware of the power of the subconscious mind, which can be programmed for success by the conscious mind through visualization, commitment and reinforcement, emotionalization, and believing. However, the path to success also requires action.

To move forward, we must also deal with denial, face the reality of our situation, and accept responsibility for ourselves and our problems. While fear, poor health, or unhealthy life choices can hold us back, embracing the right attitudes and values can release those brakes, and with empowerment skills and strategies we can accelerate our development. Understanding the law of attraction and how visualizing our goals can help manifest them—as well as the importance of money management—are also fundamental requirements of the empowerment mindset.

However, comprehension of all these principles will not have much effect unless we create a carefully conceived strategic plan based on discovering our life's purpose, developing our strategic vision, and setting our goals for the future. To succeed using the empowerment mindset, we should be mindful of an African proverb that states: "Tomorrow belongs to the people who prepare for it today."[1] And we should heed the warning of Ralph Waldo Emerson, who wrote, "Power ceases in the instant of repose; it resides in the moment of transition through action from a past to a new state."[2]

We can all use the power we possess to achieve greater success and happiness. And God—however we define the word, whatever our religion, spiritual practice, or belief—truly does help those who help themselves. Whatever we envision, plan for with expectation and commitment, and act on with determination will usually manifest—bringing us increased success and happiness.

When we embrace the empowerment mindset, we gain a powerful way of perceiving and engaging with the world that may be one of the greatest legacies for well-being that we leave our family, friends, and community. We have nothing to lose but the unnecessary baggage holding us back from using the power we all possess to become the wonderful individuals we have the potential to be. By making the empowerment mindset a way of life, we can leave our regrets behind, realize our ambitions and the dreams dearest to our hearts. We can have a song in our hearts and a bounce to our steps while using knowledge from the empowerment mindset on a new path to success and happiness.

THE EMPOWERMENT MINDSET

Understand the law of correspondence:
outer world corresponds to inner world.

Commit to action through a strategic plan.

Program your subconscious mind to help you achieve success.

Visualize steps needed to move forward.

Focus on what you can change: you.

Realize that you cannot transcend what you don't confront.

NOTES

Introduction

1. Daniel Goleman, *Emotional Intelligence* (New York: Bantam Books, 1995).
2. Coleman Barks, trans., "Prayer to Be Changed," *The Soul of Rumi: A New Collection of Ecstatic Poems* (New York: HarperCollins, 2001), 152.

Chapter 1

1. John Dewey, *Democracy and Education: An Introduction to the Philosophy of Education* (New York: MacMillan, 1930), 408, http://bit.ly/z6qgtz.
2. http://thinkexist.com/quotation/living_a_life_is_like_constructing_a_buildingif/ 338142.html or http://www.great-quotes.com/quote/625678.
3. Wayne W. Dyer, *Excuses Begone! How to Change Lifelong Self-Defeating Thinking Habits* (Carlsbad, CA: Hay House, 2009), 15.
4. Calvin Helin, *The Economic Dependency Trap: Breaking Free to Self-Reliance* (St. Louis: Ravencrest Publishing, 2011), 128.
5. Brian Tracy, *Reinvention: How to Make the Rest of Your Life the Best of Your Life* (New York: AMACOM, 2009), 19–20.
6. Ibid., 37.
7. Napoleon Hill, *Grow Rich with Peace of Mind* (New York: Penguin, 2007), 10–15.
8. Dyer, *Excuses Begone!*, 19.
9. Ibid., 20.
10. Viktor E. Frankl, *Man's Search for Meaning* (Boston: Beacon Press, 1992), 123, http://thinkexist.com/quotes/viktor_frankl/.
11. http://thinkexist.com/quotes/charles_r._swindoll/ or http://www.brainyquote.com/quotes/authors/c/charles_r_swindoll.html.
12. As cited by Jack Canfield (with Jane Switzer), *The Success Principles: How to Get from Where You Are to Where You Want to Be* (New York: HarperCollins, 2005), 6.

Chapter 2

1. James Allen, *As a Man Thinketh and From Power to Poverty* (New York: Penguin Group: 2008), 5–6.
2. Tracy, *Reinvention*, 37–38.
3. Joseph Murphy, *Amazing Laws of Cosmic Power* (New York: Penguin, 2001), 51.
4. Misty Harris, "Bitter Attitude Doesn't Do the Body Good," *The Vancouver Sun*, August 10, 2011, B1, reporting on Michael Linden and Andreas Maercker, *Embitterment: Societal, Psychological, and Clinical Perspectives*, http://www.globalnews.ca/health/health/6442461674/story.html or

http://www.sciencedaily.com/releases/2011/08/110809104259.htm.

5. http://www.rwe.org/complete-works/ii---essays-i/iii-compensation.

6. http://en.wikipedia.org/wiki/Learned_helplessness.

7. http://www.urbandictionary.com/define.php?term=self-pity.

8. Krista Tippet, *Einstein's God: Conversation about Science and the Human Spirit* (New York: Penguin, 2006), 228–29.

9. Ibid., 227.

10. Ibid., 229.

11. http://www.nacbt.org/whatiscbt.htm.

12. Ibid.

13. http://thinkexist.com/quotations/commitment/2.html.

14. Hill, *Grow Rich with Peace of Mind*, 36.

15. Ibid.

Chapter 3

1. http://quotationsbook.com/quote/12157/.

2. http://quotationsbook.com/quote/12144/.

3. http://quotingquotes.com/9857/ or http://www.goodreads.com/quotes/show_tag?name=ego.

Chapter 4

1. John Briggs, PhD, and F. David Peat, PhD, *Seven Lessons of Chaos: Timely Wisdom for the Science of Change* (New York: HarperCollins, 1999), 20.

2. Ibid.

3. "The Largest English-Speaking Country? China, of Course," *Irish Times*, http://www.irishtimes.com/newspaper/weekend/2009/0620/1224249169396.html.

4. This presentation was originally prepared for a Sony Corporation executive conference, and the original content owner is Sony Music Entertainment. http://www.youtube.com/watch?v=cL9Wu2kWwSY, http://www.huffingtonpost.com/2009/03/30/did-you-know-crazy-facts_n_180663.html, http://bit.ly/yl6vrg or http://www.youtube.com/watch?v=sMTzTX7lEKM, or http://bit.ly/AAHLSB. All information provided in this and the following paragraph on the rapid rate of technological change is derived from these sources except where additional sources are noted.

5. Ibid.

6. Gillian Butler, PhD, and Tony Hope, MD, *Managing Your Mind: The Mental Fitness Guide*, 2nd ed. (New York: Oxford University Press, 2007), 22.

7. http://www.brainyquote.com/quotes/quotes/h/helenkelle121787.html.

8. Tracy, *Reinvention*, 29–30.

9. http://www.special-dictionary.com/quotes/authors/m/myrtle_reed/112907.htm.

Chapter 5

1. http://www.thefreedictionary.com/mind.
2. http://www.dictionary-quotes.com/the-only-person-you-are-destined-to-become-is-the-person-you-decide-to-be-ralph-waldo-emerson/.

Chapter 6

1. http://www.quotationspage.com/quote/30187.html.
2. http://thinkexist.com/quotation/the_heart_has_reasons_that_reason_does_not/196041.html.
3. http://quotationsbook.com/quote/18821/#axzz1Cyrd1gFO.
4. Butler and Hope, *Managing Your Mind*, 17.
5. New International Version, http://www.topverses.com/?verse=16514.
6. http://www.vcu.edu/engweb/transcendentalism/ideas/rosecrans.html.
7. http://www.starstuffs.com/prayers/.
8. Ibid.
9. http://www.prayeroftheheart.com/POHMethod.html.
10. http://www.prayerguide.org.uk/stfrancis.html.
11. http://buddhistfaith.tripod.com/buddhistprayer/id5.html.
12. http://mysteryofiniquity.wordpress.com/2006/12/06/ralph-waldo-emerson-on-prayer/.
13. http://www.towardtheone.com/prayers.htm.
14. Ibid.

Chapter 7

1. http://quotationsbook.com/quote/34502/.
2. http://www.rwe.org/complete-works/ii---essays-i/iii-compensation.
3. http://viewonbuddhism.org/karma.html.
4. As cited at http://viewonbuddhism.org/karma.html.
5. Craig and Marc Kielburger, *From Me to We: Turning Self-Help on Its Head* (Mississauga, Ontario: John Wiley & Sons Canada, 2004), 81–82.

Chapter 8

1. http://en.wikipedia.org/wiki/Consciousness.
2. http://www.merriam-webster.com/dictionary/subconscious.
3. http://en.wikipedia.org/wiki/Unconscious_mind.
4. http://www.medicalnewstoday.com/releases/18022.php5.
5. http://www.nytimes.com/2007/07/31/health/31iht-snpriming.1.6916871.html.
6. *American Speaker: Your Guide to Successful Speaking* (Washington: Georgetown Publishing House, 1996), BOD/4.
7. Ibid., BOD/3.

8. Canfield, *The Success Principles*, 83.

9. Ibid., 81.

10. Ibid., 82–83. Canfield suggests that the RAS functions like a filter, only letting in information that is critical to survival, including anything that will help one achieve goals that they visualize and affirm, saying, "When you give your brain specific, colorful, and vividly compelling pictures to manifest—it will seek out and capture all the information necessary to bring that picture up into reality for you."

11. Brian Tracy, *Goals! How to Get Everything You Want—Faster Than You Ever Thought Possible* (San Francisco: Berrett-Koehler, 2004), 62.

12. Canfield, *The Success Principles*, 81–82.

13. Ibid.

14. http://sportsmedicine.about.com/cs/sport_psych/a/aa091700a.htm.

15. As recounted by Canfield in *The Success Principles*, 82.

16. http://www.rodneyohebsion.com/napoleon-hill.htm.

17. http://www.merriam-webster.com/dictionary/belief.

18. http://www.essortment.com/creative-visualization-techniques-63857.html.

19. http://dictionary.reference.com/browse/actualize.

Chapter 9

1. http://en.wikipedia.org/wiki/Spirit.

2. http://www.answers.com/topic/spirit.

3. http://en.wikipedia.org/wiki/Spirit.

4. http://bible.cc/matthew/10-28.htm.

5. "Animism," *The Columbia Encyclopedia*, 6th ed., 2000–2007, http://www.encyclopedia.com/topic/animism.aspx.

6. http://en.wikipedia.org/wiki/Reincarnation#Taoism. Original source: Herbert A. Giles, *Chuang Tzu: Mystic, Moralist, and Social Reformer* (London: Bernard and Quatrich, 1889), 304, http://books.google.com/books?id=vMNI-aFtF4UC&printsec=frontcover#v=onepage&q&f=false.

7. http://www.famous-quotes.com/topic.php?tid=579.

8. Ibid.

9. http://quotationsbook.com/quote/19598/#axzz1Cs5VKumv.

10. http://www.orientaloutpost.com/shufa.php?q=fighting%20spirit.

11. http://www.famousquotesandauthors.com/authors/david_v__a__ambrose_quotes.html.

Chapter 10

1. http://www.quotesdaddy.com/quote/519/a-p-gouthev/to-get-profit-without-risk-experience-without-danger.

2. http://thinkexist.com/quotation/failure_should_be_our_teacher-not_our_undertaker/13142.html.

3. http://en.wikipedia.org/wiki/Nothing_to_Fear_But_Fear_Itself.

4. Hill, *Grow Rich with Peace of Mind*, 47.

5. Ibid., 39.

6. Murphy, *Amazing Laws of Cosmic Power*, 123, http://www.famousquotesandauthors.com/authors/dale_carnegie_quotes.html.

7. http://www.quotegarden.com/risk.html.

8. William Shakespeare, *Measure for Measure*, Act I, scene 4, http://www.quotationspage.com/quote/25216.html.

9. Nathaniel Branden, *Taking Responsibility: Self-Reliance and the Accountable Life* (New York: Simon & Schuster, 1996), 70.

10. Hill, *Grow Rich with Peace of Mind*, 24–25.

11. Ibid.

12. http://www.brainyquote.com/quotes/quotes/f/franklind122780.html.

13. http://www.quotationspage.com/quote/29333.html.

14. http://www.brainyquote.com/quotes/quotes/j/johndewey121337.html.

Chapter 13

1. Ken Seeley with Myatt Murphy, *Face It and Fix It: A Three-Step Plan to Break Free from Denial and Discover the Life You Deserve* (New York: HarperCollins, 2009), 10–11.

2. Ibid., 17.

Chapter 14

1. http://thinkexist.com/quotation/you_must_take_personal_responsibility-you_cannot/212318.html.

Chapter 15

1. Lewis Carroll, *Through the Looking Glass* (New York: Signet, 2000), 64.

2. http://www.peak22.com/peak22/P703-workbook-1.pdf.

3. http://www.scribd.com/doc/2053084/Purpose-Vision-Goals.

4. Tracy, *Reinvention*, 10–11.

5. Canfield, *The Success Principles*, 21.

6. Ibid., 19.

7. Ibid., 22–23. Canfield cites the source of this version of the Life Purpose exercise as Arnold M. Patent, spiritual coach and author of *You Can Have It All*.

8. http://www.peak22.com/peak22/P703-workbook-1.pdf.

Chapter 16

1. http://www.scribd.com/doc/2053084/Purpose-Vision-Goals.

2. http://www.selfgrowth.com/articles/Peterkin3.html.

3. http://www.squidoo.com/personal-vision-statement.

4. Ibid.

Chapter 17

1. Brian Tracy, *Flight Plan: The Real Secret of Success* (San Francisco: Berrett-Koehler Publishers, 2008), 36.

2. Ibid.

3. Ibid.

Conclusion

1. http://thinkexist.com/quotation/for_tomorrow_belongs_to_the_people_who_prepare/174510.html.

2. Ralph Waldo Emerson, *Self-Reliance* (White Plains, NY: Peter Pauper Press, 1967), 59.

BIBLIOGRAPHY

Articles and Books

Allen, James. *As a Man Thinketh and From Power to Poverty.* New York: Penguin, 2008.

American Speaker: Your Guide to Successful Speaking (Washington, DC: Georgetown Publishing House, 1996), BOD/4.

Barks, Coleman, trans. *The Soul of Rumi: A New Collection of Ecstatic Poems.* New York: HarperCollins, 2001.

Branden, Nathaniel. *Taking Responsibility: Self-Reliance and the Accountable Life.* New York: Simon & Schuster, 1996.

Briggs, John, and F. David Peat. *Seven Lessons of Chaos: Timely Wisdom for the Science of Change.* New York: HarperCollins, 1999.

Butler, Gillian, and Tony Hope. *Managing Your Mind: The Mental Fitness Guide*, 2nd ed. New York: Oxford University Press, 2007.

Canfield, Jack (with Jane Switzer). *The Success Principles: How to Get from Where You Are to Where You Want to Be.* New York: HarperCollins, 2005.

Carroll, Lewis. *Through the Looking Glass.* New York: Signet, 2000.

Dewey, John. *Democracy and Education: An Introduction to the Philosophy of Education.* New York: MacMillan, 1930.

Dyer, Wayne W. *Excuses Begone! How to Change Lifelong Self-Defeating Thinking Habits.* Carlsbad, CA: Hay House, 2009.

Emerson, Ralph Waldo. *Self-Reliance.* White Plains, NY: Peter Pauper Press, 1967, 2008.

Frankl, Viktor E. *Man's Search for Meaning.* Boston: Beacon Press, 1992.

Giles, Herbert A. *Chuang Tzu: Mystic, Moralist, and Social Reformer.* London: Bernard and Quatrich, 1889.

Goleman, Daniel. *Emotional Intelligence.* New York: Bantam Books, 1995.

Helin, Calvin. *The Economic Dependency Trap: Breaking Free to Self-Reliance.* St. Louis: Ravencrest Publishing, 2011.

Hill, Napoleon. *Grow Rich with Peace of Mind.* New York: Penguin, 2007.

Kielburger, Craig and Marc. *From Me to We: Turning Self-Help on Its Head.* Mississauga, Ontario. John Wiley & Sons Canada, 2004.

Linden, Michael, and Andreas Maercker. *Embitterment: Societal, Psychological and Clinical Perspectives.* New York: SpringerWien, 2011.

Murphy, Joseph. *Amazing Laws of Cosmic Power.* New York: Penguin, 2001.

Seeley, Ken, and Myatt Murphy. *Face It and Fix It: A Three-Step Plan to Break Free from Denial and Discover the Life You Deserve.* New York: HarperCollins, 2009.

Seligman, M. E. P. *Helplessness: On Depression, Development, and Death.* San Francisco: W. H. Freeman, 1975.

Shakespeare, William. *Measure for Measure*. Charleston, SC: Forgotten Books, 2008.

Solomon, Andrew. *The Noonday Demon: An Atlas of Depression*. New York: Scribner, 2001.

Tippet, Krista. *Einstein's God: Conversations about Science and the Human Spirit*. New York: Penguin, 2006.

Tracy, Brian. *Flight Plan: The Real Secret of Success*. San Francisco: Berrett-Koehler, 2008.

Tracy, Brian. *Goals! How to Get Everything You Want—Faster Than You Ever Thought Possible*. San Francisco: Berrett-Koehler Publishers, 2003.

Tracy, Brian. *Reinvention: How to Make the Rest of Your Life the Best of Your Life*. New York: AMACOM, 2009.

Newspapers

Harris, Misty. "Bitter Attitude Doesn't Do the Body Good." *The Vancouver Sun*, August 10, 2011, B1.

Online Sources

http://www.answers.com/topic/spirit.

http://bible.cc/matthew/10-28.htm.

http://bit.ly/AAHLSB.

http://bit.ly/oN2Oa9.

http://bit.ly/yl6vrg.

http://bit.ly/z6qgtz.

http://books.google.com/books?id=vMNI-aFtF4UC&printsec=frontcover#v=onepage&q&f=false.

http://www.brainyquote.com/quotes/authors/c/charles_r_swindoll.html.

http://www.brainyquote.com/quotes/quotes/f/franklind122780.html.

http://www.brainyquote.com/quotes/quotes/h/helenkelle121787.html.

http://www.brainyquote.com/quotes/quotes/j/johndewey121337.html.

http://buddhistfaith.tripod.com/buddhistprayer/id5.html.

http://www.dictionary-quotes.com/the-only-person-you-are-destined-to-become-is-the-person-you-decide-to-be-ralph-waldo-emerson/.

http://dictionary.reference.com/browse/actualize.

http://www.encyclopedia.com/topic/animism.aspx.

http://en.wikipedia.org/wiki/Consciousness.

http://en.wikipedia.org/wiki/Learned_helplessness.

http://en.wikipedia.org/wiki/Nothing_to_Fear_But_Fear_Itself.

http://en.wikipedia.org/wiki/Spirit.

http://en.wikipedia.org/wiki/Reincarnation#Taoism.

http://en.wikipedia.org/wiki/Unconscious_mind.

http://www.essortment.com/creative-visualization-techniques-63857.html.

http://www.famousquotesandauthors.com/authors/david_v__a__ambrose_quotes.html.

http://www.famousquotesandauthors.com/authors/dale_carnegie_quotes.html.

http://www.famous-quotes.com/topic.php?tid=579.

http://www.globalnews.ca/health/health/6442461674/story.html.

http://www.goodreads.com/quotes/show_tag?name=ego.

http://www.great-quotes.com/quote/625678.

http://www.huffingtonpost.com/2009/03/30/did-you-know-crazy-facts_n_180663.html.

http://www.irishtimes.com/newspaper/weekend/2009/0620/1224249169396.html.

http://www.medicalnewstoday.com/releases/18022.php5.

http://www.merriam-webster.com/dictionary/belief.

http://www.merriam-webster.com/dictionary/subconscious.

http://mysteryofiniquity.wordpress.com/2006/12/06/ralph-waldo-emerson-on-prayer/.

http://www.nacbt.org/whatiscbt.htm.

http://www.nytimes.com/2007/07/31/health/31iht-snpriming.1.6916871.html?page
   wanted=1&_r=1.

http://www.orientaloutpost.com/shufa.php?q=fighting%20spirit.

http://www.peak22.com/peak22/P703-workbook-1.pdf.

http://www.prayerguide.org.uk/stfrancis.html.

http://www.prayeroftheheart.com/POHMethod.html.

http://quotationsbook.com/quote/12157/.

http://quotationsbook.com/quote/12144/.

http://quotationsbook.com/quote/18821/#axzz1Cyrd1gFO.

http://quotationsbook.com/quote/19598/#axzz1Cs5VKumv.

http://quotationsbook.com/quote/34502/.

http://www.quotesdaddy.com/quote/519/a-p-gouthev/to-get-profit-without-risk-experience-
   without-danger.

http://www.quotegarden.com/risk.html.

http://www.quotationspage.com/quote/25216.html.

http://www.quotationspage.com/quote/29333.html.

http://www.quotationspage.com/quote/30187.html.

http://quotingquotes.com/9857/.

http://www.rodneyohebsion.com/napoleon-hill.htm.

http://www.rwe.org/complete-works/ii---essays-i/iii-compensation.

http://www.sciencedaily.com/releases/2011/08/110809104259.htm.

http://www.scribd.com/doc/2053084/Purpose-Vision-Goals.

http://www.selfgrowth.com/articles/Peterkin3.html.

http://www.shudokan.ca/.

http://www.special-dictionary.com/quotes/authors/m/myrtle_reed/112907.htm.

http://sportsmedicine.about.com/cs/sport_psych/a/aa091700a.htm.

http://www.squidoo.com/personal-vision-statement.

http://www.starstuffs.com/prayers/.

http://www.thefreedictionary.com/mind.

http://thinkexist.com/quotes/charles_r._swindoll/.

http://thinkexist.com/quotations/commitment/2.html.

http://thinkexist.com/quotation/failure_should_be_our_teacher-not_our_undertaker/
13142.html.

http://thinkexist.com/quotation/for_tomorrow_belongs_to_the_people_who_prepare/
174510.html.

http://thinkexist.com/quotation/live_as_if_your_were_to_die_tomorrow-learn_as_if/
253507.html.

http://thinkexist.com/quotation/living_a_life_is_like_constructing_a_building-if/338142.html.

http://thinkexist.com/quotation/the_heart_has_reasons_that_reason_does_not/196041.html.

http://thinkexist.com/quotes/viktor_frankl/.

http://thinkexist.com/quotation/you_must_take_personal_responsibility-you_cannot/
212318.html.

http://www.topverses.com/?verse=16514.

http://www.towardtheone.com/prayers.htm.

http://www.urbandictionary.com/define.php?term=self-pity.

http://www.vcu.edu/engweb/transcendentalism/ideas/rosecrans.html.

http://viewonbuddhism.org/karma.html.

http://www.youtube.com/watch?v=cL9Wu2kWwSY.

http://www.youtube.com/watch?v=sMTzTX7lEKM.

INDEX

Accountability, 29, 32, 98, 124
    choosing, 44
    countering emotional and
        mental sabotage, 41–42
    facing reality, 135
    freedom from group-
        conditioned negativity, 41
    taking personal responsibility,
        133(fig.)
Action orientation, 114(fig.)
Actions and actualization, 87–89
    being proactive, 114(fig.),
        118
    chain of causation leading to
        destiny, 106(fig.)
    conscious mind, 76(fig.)
    formation of the self, 27–29
    importance in achieving
        goals, 118
    law of attraction, 112–113,
        113(fig.)
    process of reinvention, 61(fig.)
    strategic vision, 154, 156,
        157(fig.)
    subconscious and conscious
        minds, 77(fig.), 78
Affirmations, 30–31, 32, 41–
    42, 85–86, 207
African Americans, 168–194
Alice in Wonderland (Carroll),
    147
Allen, James, 33–34, 41, 115,
    123
Ancestors, opening the heart
    with, 68
Angelou, Maya, 27, 71
Animism, 91
Aristotle, 114
Atkinson, Brooks, 98
Attitudes. See Thoughts and
    attitudes

Attraction, law of, 111–112,
    117, 118, 212
Augustine (saint), 91

Beliefs. See Values and beliefs
Believing in goals, 80(fig.), 87,
    113(fig.), 154, 156,
    157(fig.), 164
Biblical references, 64, 91, 111
Bossuel, Jacques Begigne, 63
Branden, Nathaniel, 98
Brault, Robert, 105
Brennan, Stephen A., 160
Briggs, John, 49
Buddhism, 67, 73, 122
Budgeting, 127–128, 129(fig.),
    131
Business world, 141–142
Butler, Gillian, 52, 64

Canfield, Jack, 82, 149–150
Carnegie, Andrew, 41
Carnegie, Dale, 98
Carroll, Lewis, 147
Change, adapting to, 49–55,
    53
Character, 115–116
Children. See also Family and
    friends
    benefits of giving, 73
    facing fears, 100
    passing on group-conditioned
        negativity, 40–41
    reincarnation, 92
Christianity: prayer and the
    open heart, 67
Churchill, Winston, 27, 97
Cognitive-behavioral therapy
    (CBT), 37–38

Comfort zone, 51
Commitment and reinforce-
    ment, 80–81, 80(fig.), 85–86,
    113(fig.), 157(fig.), 160,
    161, 163, 164, 172–173
Communicate, ability to, 125,
    130
Communities and neighbor-
    hoods, 65(fig.), 73–74, 171
Community- and group-
    conditioned negativity, 38–41,
    43
Compensation for giving, 73–74
Conscious mind, 75–90
    about, 75–76
    defining, 57, 89
    development of habitual
        thought patterns, 59
    reincarnation, 92
    subconscious and, 30–31,
        77(fig.), 79(fig.), 83(fig.),
        89
Constructive action, 58
Control, 36, 38–39, 52
Cortés, Hernán, 141
Cosman, E. Joseph, 133
Creative conscious mind, 30
Crying, 64

Dalai Lama, 73
Darwin, Charles, 49, 50
Denial, 133(fig.), 134,
    211–212
Depression, 37
Despair, 68
Destiny, 106(fig.), 117,
    141–142
Dewey, John, 27
DJ Bionic Dave, 94–95

Dreams and dreaming, 71–72, 187

Dyer, Wayne W., 27, 29, 30, 149

Edison, Thomas, 41

Education
acquiring skills and strategies, 124–128
learning from failure, 98–100
as part of ongoing growth, 211
strategic vision scenario, 170–184, 187–188, 190–191, 195–196
visualization improving performance, 82

Ego, 45–48
diminishing the impact of, 48
habitual thought patterns developing from, 59
impact on the individual, 47(fig.), 110
open heart attitude, 64
undermining ability to succeed, 48

Einstein, Albert, 105

Embitterment research, 34

Emerson, Ralph Waldo, 34, 59, 66, 72, 212

Emotional sabotage, 34–36, 41–42, 44

Emotionalization, 80(fig.), 86, 164, 172–173
defining goals, 159
law of attraction, 112, 113(fig.)
life purpose, 185–186
open heart attitude, 63–70
programming the subconscious mind, 80–81
scenario for determining strategic vision, 170–171
strategic vision, 154, 156, 157(fig.)

Empathy, 46–48, 72

Empowerment mindset, cultivating, 213

Empty mind, 60–61

Event+response=outcome, 31

Expectations, 123–124, 128, 154

External influences, 52, 80(fig.)

Fabry, Joseph, 92

Failure, 97–101
acceptance of, 17–18
controlling formation of the self, 27, 29
ego causing aversion to risk, 46
lateral violence stemming from feelings of, 37
learning how to fail, 101
mental and emotional sabotage, 42
overcoming fears about, 99(fig.)
passing on group-conditioned negativity, 40–41
subconscious programming to reverse, 31

Family and friends. See also Children
facing fears, 100
habitual thought patterns, 59
open heart development, 68
passing on group-conditioned negativity, 40–41
providing hope and inspiration, 71–72
strategic plan involving, 168, 170–173, 184–185, 187–188, 193–194
trust, 64, 65(fig.)

Fear, 97–101, 121
existence of the subconscious mind, 78
facing and overcoming, 100, 101
habitual thought patterns, 59
and inaction, 58
open heart attitude, 63–64
overcoming fears about failure, 99(fig.)
of the unknown, 52–53

Fight-or-flight response, 77

Financial literacy, 126–128, 129(fig.), 131

Flight Plan (Tracy), 159

Focus, ability to, 124, 130

Ford, Henry, 41

Francis of Assisi (saint), 67

Frankl, Viktor E., 30

Freud, Sigmund, 80

From Me to We: Turning Self-Help on Its Head (Kielburger and Kielburger), 74

Frost, Robert, 17

Fundamentals of empowerment, 121–131

Gandhi, Mohandas "Mahatma," 57, 87

Garfield, Charles A., 81

Giving, growing through, 71–74

Giving, law of, 72, 74

Goals. See also Actions and actualization; Emotionalization; Visualization
activating the law of attraction, 117
believing in, 87
commitment and reinforcement, 85–86
establishing, 161, 172–173, 188–190
focus on, 124
group-conditioned negativity defeating achievement of, 39
identifying, 160–164
importance of, 164
mindstorming, 178–180
prioritization, 124
programming the subconscious, 78
projecting forward, 180–184
qualitatively and quantatively defining, 159–160, 164
strategic plan, 143(fig.)

strategic vision, life purpose, and, 144, 148–149, 153–154, 155(fig.), 166
strategic vision scenario, 170–171

Goals! (Tracy), 159

Gouthey, A.P., 97

Gratitude, 107, 116

Growth, law of, 49–55

Habits, 114–115, 115–116, 116(fig.), 118

Habitual mind, 27, 29, 97

Habitual thought patterns, 58, 59–61, 61–62

Happiness, 63, 131

Health, powers of, 122, 128

Helplessness, learned, 36

Hill, Napoleon, 30, 41, 86, 97–98, 159

Holtmann, Christian, 94

Hope, Tony, 52, 64

Howard, Vernon, 33

Human spirit, power of, 91–96

Humility, 46, 48, 107, 116

Humphrey, Hubert, 92

Illness, physical, 34

Impressions, 81–82

Inner growth through open heart attitude, 64–65

Integrity and honesty, 108, 116

Japanese philosophy of giving, 74

Joy, impermanence as, 53

Jung, Carl, 45

Karma, 73

Keller, Helen, 53, 63

Kennedy, John F., 81, 100

Kielburger, Craig and Marc, 74

Kierkegaard, Søren, 134

Kindness, 109, 117

Lateral violence, 37

Laws of empowerment, 19

Learned helplessness, 36

Life purpose, 121–122, 128, 143(fig.), 147–152, 154, 165, 166, 185–186
strategic plan and, 142–144, 168–169
strategic vision, goals, and, 148–149, 153–154, 155(fig.), 166

Lincoln, Abraham, 108(fig.)

Locke, John, 109

Lombardi, Vince, 39

Love: open heart attitude, 64

Major definite purpose, 160

Managing Your Mind: The Mental Fitness Guide (Butler and Hope), 52, 64

Martial arts, 68, 73, 84

Martial spirit, 95

Material wealth, 64, 66, 71, 72, 123, 126–127, 130, 144

Mehrabian, Albert, 81

Mental sabotage, 34–36, 41–42, 44

Milton, John, 33

Mind, defining, 57

Mind of reinvention, 57–62

Mindstorming about goals, 163, 178–180, 199–202

Money. *See* Material wealth

Murphy, Joseph, 34

Music, 69–70, 94

Naisbitt, John, 153

Narcissism, 66

Native Americans
benefits of giving, 71–72
opening the heart through music, 69–70

power of the human spirit, 92–94

prayer and the open heart, 66
reincarnation, 92

Negative emotions, 33–44, 97, 98

Networking skills, 126

Nicklaus, Jack, 84

Nightingale, Earl, 75

Nixon, Richard, 81

Nomada, Toshiaki, 73

Nonhabitual mind, 30

The Noonday Demon: An Atlas of Depression (Solomon), 37

Open heart attitude, 63–70

Open mind, 59–63

Organizing information, 162, 163, 176–177, 195–199

Owning your problems, 133(fig.), 135–136

Paracelsus, Philius A., 92

Peat, F. David, 49

Perseverance, 109, 117, 123–124

Pessimism, 59

Peterkin, Cecile, 154

Potlatch, 72

Prayer, 66–68, 70

Primary goal, 160, 162, 164, 165, 172–176, 188–195

Prioritization, 124, 130

Proactivity, 114(fig.), 118

Proctor, Bob, 154

Programming the subconscious mind, 31, 75, 80(fig.). *See also* Conscious mind
actualization, 87–89
believing, 87
commitment and reinforcement, 85–86
determining and realizing a strategic vision, 154–155

emotionalization, 86
role of thoughts in, 111
steps of, 88(fig.), 89
synchronization of the
subconscious with the con-
scious mind, 79(fig.)
visualization, 81–85
Projecting goals forward, 163,
180–184, 202–207
Psychological barriers, 133–136

Reaction to life, 30–31, 32
Reality, 45, 48, 49, 52–55,
133(fig.), 134–135
Receptivity, 58
Redneck, Robert, 31
Reed, Myrtle, 53
Reincarnation, 92
Reinvention, 53, 57–62,
61(fig.), 211
Religion and spirituality, 66–70
existence of the soul, 91–92
materialism and, 127
prayer, 66–68
Responsibility. See Accounta-
bility
Reticular activating system
(RAS), 82
Risk, 46, 97–101
Rohn, Jim, 141
Roosevelt, Franklin D., 97, 100
Rumi, 20

Sabotage, emotional, 34–36,
41–42, 44
Sabotage, mental, 34–36,
41–42, 44
Saint-Exupéry, Antoine de, 63
Secret orders, 149–150
Seeley, Ken, 134
Self, formation of, 27, 29
Self-absorption, 45
Self-defeating behavior, 33, 44
Self-discipline, 125, 127, 130

Self-esteem, 36
Self-love. See Ego
Self-pity, 36
Self-reflection, 60–61
Self-responsibility, 32
Self-worth, 123
Seneca, 135, 147
Sensory cues, 78
Seven Life Lessons of Chaos
(Briggs and Peat), 49
Shakespeare, William, 98
Sinclair, Adlin, 124
Skills and strategies, acquiring,
124–129
Social structure, Darwinian
view of, 49
Solomon, Andrew, 37
Soul, 91
Spirit lifters, 69(fig.)
Spiritual warriors, 91, 94–95,
141
Sports performance, 82
Stable element in our lives,
149(fig.)
Static view of reality, 53–55
Stone, W. Clement, 87
Strategic plan, 141–145
establishing goals, 159–164,
188–190
importance of, 165, 212
life purpose, 147–152, 168
169, 185–186
mindstorming, 178–180,
199–202
organizing information,
176–178, 195–199
primary goal, 173–176,
190–195
projecting goals forward,
180–184, 202–207
steps toward making, 168–
207
strategic vision and, 153–
158, 186–188

Strategic vision, 143(fig.), 145,
165, 212
determining and realizing,
157(fig.)
developing, 153–158
life purpose, goals and,
148–149, 155(fig.), 166
scenario for determining,
170–171, 186–188
statement of, 166
Strength of mind, 109
Subconscious mind, 75–90,
76(fig.), 77(fig.). See also
Programming
conscious mind program-
ming for success, 30–31
defining and explaining,
76–79, 89
importance of awareness of,
211
imprinting goals, 160, 162,
162(box)
information flow to, 83(fig.)
programming, 27, 29, 88
synchronization with the
conscious mind, 79(fig.),
89
Success and well-being, 36, 55,
97
Success-conscious mind, 30, 32
Sustained efforts, 123–124
Swindoll, Charles R., 30–31
Synergies, 126, 130

Take action toward goals, 160,
161, 163
Taoism, 92
Tears, 64
Technology, rate of change and,
50, 52
Ten-Goal Method, 160, 162,
164
Thoughts and attitudes. See
also Negative emotions;
Toxic thoughts; WSC
(woulda, shoulda, coulda)
syndrome

chain of causation determining destiny, 117
choosing, 30
cognitive-behavioral therapy, 37–38
formation of the self, 27–29
habits undermining empowerment, 114–115
importance of, 116
law of attraction and, 111–112
open heart, 63–70
role and impact of, 105–109, 109–111
role of values in, 105–109
switching negative to positive thoughts, 117
win/win perspective, 125, 130
Toxic thoughts, 29–30, 33–44, 98, 109–111. *See also* WSC (woulda, shoulda, coulda) syndrome
Tracy, Brian, 29–30, 34, 53, 75, 159
Trust, 64, 65(fig.), 107–108, 116
Tuccaro, Dave, Jr., 92–95

Uncertainty, 58

Values and beliefs
determining a strategic vision, 170–171
habitual thought patterns, 59–60
importance of, 116
role in determining thoughts, 105–109
strategic vision statement, 166, 187
Verbal abuse, 40
Verbal impressions, 81
Victim mentality, 35–36
Violence, lateral, 37
Vision statement, 156
Visual impressions, 81–82
Visualization, 80(fig.), 81–85
defining goals, 159–164
formation of the self, 27–29
information flow to the subconscious mind, 83(fig.)
law of attraction, 113(fig.)
life purpose, 185–186
strategic vision, 157(fig.), 170–171
subconscious mind and, 75, 77(fig.), 80–81
Vocal impressions, 81

Waitley, Denis, 97
Ward, William Arthur, 165
Whitman, Harold Thurman, 121
Wilde, Oscar, 134
Win/win perspective, 125, 130
WSC (woulda, shoulda, coulda) syndrome, 18–19, 21
chain of causation leading to destiny, 106(fig.)
countering emotional and mental sabotage, 42
denial, 134
depression stemming from, 37
developing open-mindedness, 60–61
facing fears, 100
facing reality, 134–135
mental sabotage, 34–36
power of thought, 111
risk taking, 46
strategic vision, 144

Yunus, Muhammad, 211

Ziglar, Zig, 85

ABOUT THE AUTHOR

Calvin Helin, a member of the Native American Tsimshian Nation and son of a hereditary chief, works as an attorney and entrepreneur. Helin has written several publications on law, indigenous business, and associated issues, and has developed an international reputation through his best-selling book, *Dances with Dependency: Out of Poverty through Self-Reliance*. With the more recent release of his multi-award-winning book, *The Economic Dependency Trap: Breaking Free to Self-Reliance*, Helin has an expanding international role as a popular public speaker and thought leader. His commonsense messages of empowerment, self-reliance, and self-responsibility are now being promoted on a global platform.

Helin runs business enterprises that include the Eagle Group of Companies and the Native Investment and Trade Association, and is associate counsel with the law firm Stewart, Aulinger & Company. He holds directorships on the Vancouver Board of Trade, where he chairs the newly formed Aboriginal Opportunities Committee, GeoScience BC, and the Canada–China Resource Development Foundation. In addition to numerous national and regional distinctions, he has received "Top 40 Under 40" awards for both British Columbia and nationally for Canada. He has served as chairman of a recent Aboriginal trade delegation to China and introduced an innovative business model to promote long-term benefits to indigenous people from natural resource development.

Helin also serves as an ambassador for SOS Children's Village BC, a nonprofit providing a safe foster care environment for vulnerable children, and is a member of the Advisory Council of the prestigious think tank the MacDonald-Laurier Institute. A third-degree black belt, he teaches at the Shudokan Karate and Education Society, a group he founded in 2002 that provides free martial arts lessons to empower disadvantaged inner-city children by educating them in discipline, manners, self-respect, and other important life lessons. Empowerment through knowledge has been a theme central to all of Helin's activities.

Made in the USA
San Bernardino, CA
30 December 2012